Praise for THE MASTER PLAN

Through the pages of THE MASTER PLAN, Mike has become an important voice in answering the question that is "top of mind" for so many of today's generation of leaders: "What must I do to rise above mere success to achieve true significance?" The message of Mike's book is profoundly simple...be a leader who cares about others, who commits to others, and who gives to others.

This book is rich with personal stories that will guide you on your path to success and fuel your passion to realize significance in every aspect of your leadership journey.

—**John C. Maxwell**
Best Selling Author of
THE 21 IRREFUTABLE LAWS OF LEADERSHIP

• • • • •

Freedom comes from inspiration. Mike Ingram's inspiring story tells of his quest for freedom, growth, progress and advancement that will inspire every reader to live, love, and experience the American Dream!"

—**Mark Victor Hansen**
Co-creator of the CHICKEN SOUP FOR THE SOUL series

⋯⋯

I've always believed—and told anyone who would listen to me—that success is 90% attitude, and 10% other stuff.

Then I met Mike Ingram. Mike is all about attitude, attitude, attitude. The "other stuff" barely comes in second.

Mike Ingram didn't become one of the most successful men I've ever met because of what he has accomplished. His success lies in his attitudes. He has the right attitude about people. He has the right attitude about his product. He has the right attitude about power. He understands that power isn't about control. Power comes from the values that empower the individual. He understands that true power springs forth from integrity, compassion, and sacrifice for others.

This book is a special gift to you by an amazing, caring leader who has experienced the valleys and the peaks of building a business. It's destined to become a classic book of encouragement for all who want to launch or rebuild their own businesses—or discover or recapture the greatness in their lives.

—**Zig Ziglar**
From the Foreword

·····

One of the business principles that I have always tried to observe is this: "Choose your partners wisely."

This sounds very simple on the surface, but it's amazing to me how many people have fallen into the trap of forming relationships with those of questionable integrity.

After reading THE MASTER PLAN, it should become clear to you why Mike Ingram has become a trusted partner of mine in many of our mutual business ventures. Mike is a very forthright and transparent individual and I look forward to a continuing association with him.

If you desire significant success, Mike's book offers a clear and concise roadmap.

—Jerry Colangelo
Chairman, USA Basketball;
Partner, JDM Partners

•••••

If you enjoy stories of faith and perseverance—especially stories of those who keep the faith and persevere even in life's darkest times—this book will be a source of great inspiration! Through all of his ups and downs, Mike Ingram has never failed to "walk the talk." He cares deeply and sincerely about his family, his friends, his associates, and his investors, and he keeps on giving when most of us would say, "It's my turn to receive."

I believe it could be Mike's selflessness that has led to his success, and I am pleased to count him among my most enduring friends.

—**Stan Toler**
Best Selling author

•••••

I have always been struck by Mike's sincerity and his enthusiasm for life, and I love being with Mike, whether it's doing deals or just enjoying God's creation. I could write a short book on the many episodes that Mike and I have enjoyed in life together, but we are not through, yet. So I will wait a while to write the "rest of the story!"

There is no question that Mike is "highly favored of God," for all have witnessed the anointing that God has placed on his life with regard to his business skills, perception of opportunities, compassion for his Lord Jesus Christ, and his love for his fellow man.

Mike truly exercises the talents given to him from the Lord, and I am excited for the next adventure that we embark on together.

—**H.D. "Buddy" Bennett**

Clovis, New Mexico

• • • • •

I was introduced to Mike many years ago through a good friend of mine, Jerry Caven. Jerry had started investing with Mike and had done quite well.

At first, I was quite skeptical, as Mike seemed to be just too good of a salesman. It took me several years to figure out if he was for real. I very cautiously started investing in Mike's deals and found out that Jerry was right; this guy could make deals happen. After three or four years of making some nice returns and getting comfortable with Mike, I started getting some other people (including some of my employees) in Mike's investments.

Mike and I became not only business partners, but also good friends. We rodeo, hunt, boat, and just generally have a great time together. My wife and I always enjoy spending time with Mike and Sheila.

Mike always contributes more than his fair share in whatever he does. Here's to another 20 years!

—**Larry Williams**

· · · · ·

I have known Mike for many years. We originally met through our shared passion to support Childhelp and abused children. We discovered many shared interests and became dear friends. From investing in many of his projects, supporting many non-profits together as well as some very fun trips along the way, we have seen his incredible heart and tremendous generosity first hand. When Zig Ziglar encouraged him to write a book, I was beyond honored when Mike asked for my support. His story is one that everyone should read. It will open your mind to the true strategies for building wildly successful businesses, as well as inspire you to not only do more with what you already have, but also give more to help others along the way. You will laugh, you will cry but mostly you will be inspired by The Master Plan.

—**Sharon Lechter**
New York Times Bestselling Author

THE MASTER PLAN

*Three Keys to Building
a Business and Life with Purpose*

MIKE INGRAM
2019 recipient of the Horatio Alger Award

Foreword by
Zig Ziglar

Copyright © 2012 and 2020 by El Dorado Holdings, Inc.

All rights reserved.

With the exception of brief quotations used in reviews, no part of this book may be copied, reproduced or transmitted by any means, including photocopying, radio or television broadcasts, newspaper or magazine reports, motion pictures, Internet Web pages, emails, audio or video recordings of any type, or digital or microfilm storage and retrieval systems.

LCCN 2020901327

ISBN 978-1-7337706-0-6

Published in Scottsdale, Arizona by El Dorado Holdings, Inc
Printed in the USA

19 20 21 22 23 24 25 • 10 9 8 7 6 5 4 3 2 1

DEDICATION

**To my mother who gave in every possible way—
C. Maude Ingram.**

· · · · ·

My dad, Paul, was a very honorable and good man. In the thirteen years he was able to spend with me, we shared truly special father-son experiences that I will never forget. He treated me to many ball games and taught me how to hunt and fish before his untimely death at 42 years of age. He passed away after battling cancer for three years.

My mom was widowed at 36 years of age and left with a 13-year-old son who was trying to find his place in life. She was uneducated and faced a huge mortgage on a motel that my dad had built three years earlier. She also had stacks of medical bills as the result of Dad's cancer battle. She never dated another man, telling me, "No one can match your dad."

She was also concerned that another man might not treat her son with the same love and affection as he had. My mom did, however, know how to pray, and prayer was at every meal and nightly ritual. We were in church anytime the church door was open.

I never tried to test her will, and I tried to honor and accept her faith and values. She had endured more heartache and pain than anyone I know. She was truly a saint. All I can say is, "Thanks, Mom."

It was my Mom's love and example that helped shape my appreciation for the other women in my life. I attribute a lot of my success to the women who have supported me along the way. My wife Sheila has been with me every step of the way and keeps my perspective about family, faith and business real. Deb Bricker has been on this business journey from the beginning and is the foundational strength for us all. Denise Organ has been at my side and anticipates and resolves our needs before we recognize we have them.

There are so many other incredible women, whether they are in our office, are our Investors, or through our philanthropic endeavors, that without them all we would not have enjoyed or realized our Master Plan.

• • • • •

TABLE OF CONTENTS

DEDICATION		*ix*
FOREWORD	By Zig Ziglar (from the First Edition, 2012)	*1*
INTRODUCTION		*5*
BACKGROUND		*9*

THE FIRST KEY: PEOPLE POWER

One	THE POWER OF RELATIONSHIPS	*19*
Two	THE POWER OF NETWORKING	*29*
Three	THE POWER OF PARTNERSHIPS	*41*
Four	THE POWER OF TEAMWORK	*49*
Five	THE POWER OF LOYALTY	*61*
Six	THE POWER OF TRUST	*67*
Seven	THE POWER OF CUSTOMERS	*79*

THE SECOND KEY: PRODUCT POWER

Eight	THE POWER OF INNOVATION	*83*
Nine	THE POWER OF DESIGN	*93*
Ten	THE POWER OF ADDING VALUE	*101*
Eleven	THE POWER OF CREATIVE MARKETING	*107*
Twelve	THE POWER OF SERVICE	*127*

| Thirteen | THE POWER OF SCALABILITY | 133 |
| Fourteen | THE POWER OF THE MULTIPLE WIN | 143 |

THE THIRD KEY: PERSONAL POWER

Fifteen	THE POWER OF VISION	149
Sixteen	THE POWER OF ENTHUSIASM	161
Seventeen	THE POWER OF INTEGRITY	167
Eighteen	THE POWER OF FORGIVENESS	175
Nineteen	THE POWER OF PERSISTENCE	181
Twenty	THE POWER OF THINKING BIG	201
Twenty-one	THE POWER OF GIVING BACK	225
Twenty-two	THE POWER OF FREEDOM	249
Summary	THE ULTIMATE MASTER PLAN	259
Afterword	A SPECIAL P.S. TO EVERY READER AND EVERY FRIEND:	263
Acknowledgments		265
About the Author and The Horatio Alger Society		267

● ● ● ● ●

FOREWORD

Zig Ziglar

I've always believed—and told anyone who would listen to me—that success is 90% attitude, and 10% other stuff.

Then I met Mike Ingram. Mike is all about attitude, attitude, attitude. The "other stuff" barely comes in second.

Mike Ingram didn't become one of the most successful men I've ever met because of what he has accomplished. His success lies in his attitudes.

He has the right attitude about people. He knows that by building relationships, he can build a successful business and a successful life. He knows that by helping others succeed—employees, investors, and clients—everyone becomes a winner. Mike does not believe in "either/or." He believes in "all."

He has the right attitude about his product. He realizes that a successful business cannot sacrifice quality on the altar of immediate sales or short-term profit. His product is all about long-term results—satisfied investors, development partners, and customers.

He has the right attitude about power. He understands that power isn't about control. Power comes from the values that empower the individual. He understands that true power springs forth from integrity, compassion, and sacrifice for others.

Right now, you might be thinking that a man such as Mike Ingram couldn't possibly be real. That he couldn't actually exist.

Good news, friend! He is real! He does exist! I know, because I count him among my closest friends. He would probably tell you that I am his mentor, and he is my protégé. But I see just the opposite. In many respects, Mike is my mentor, and I am his protégé.

Knowledge is as individual as we are. No one can learn it all, apply it all, or teach it all. The same thing applies to wisdom. No one is "all wise." Yet, great knowledge and wisdom are available to you through the pages of this book.

Mike has used proven, time-honored techniques to build, expand, and enjoy his business and his life. He has learned how to develop a loyal customer base, how to add significant value to products and services, and how to regroup after devastating setbacks. This is a story of overcoming, whether it was surviving tough economic times or forgiving those who sought to take advantage of him. It's about following a well-designed "Master Plan."

At his core, Mike Ingram is also a "Christian" businessman. He has lost or gained more wealth than most of us will ever see. But through his experiences, he has learned to trust God. Faith is the foundation upon which his businesses have been built. You will learn valuable business principles from his life; principles that will guide you or strengthen you when you face the lions of adversity.

This book is a special gift to you by an amazing, caring leader who has experienced the valleys and the peaks of building a business. It's destined to become a classic book of encouragement for all who want to launch or rebuild their own businesses—or discover or recapture the greatness in their lives.

—**Zig Ziglar**

May, 2012, Dallas, Texas

(For the First Edition of this book.)

Zig Ziglar passed November 28, 2012, leaving an incredible library and legacy of wisdom that lives on through everyone who's life he touched. It was an honor to have his friendship and mentorship.

• • • • •

INTRODUCTION

Starting and operating a successful business is just about the toughest pursuit there is in life. In fact, I can only think of one more difficult—starting and maintaining a successful marriage!

The fact is, business and marriage have several things in common. They both require a Master Plan. They both are built on vision, commitment, and integrity. But it goes beyond that. In both business and marriage, *creativity* is essential.

Vision empowers you, your business, and your partner to set a specific goal, determine your intended direction, and work toward it. Commitment is the driving force that helps you move in your intended direction to achieve your goal. Integrity is what holds it all together.

But creativity? Well, that's the "secret sauce." It is the spice in marriage. And it is the recipe for success in business.

Creativity is what confounds your competitors, pleases your customers, amazes your investors, and inspires your team. It can take many forms and be operative in many areas of a business. It can be expressed in your product or service itself, in the way you market your product or service, and in the way you serve customers. I would venture to say that creativity is even at the foundation of loyalty—on the part of all your key "constituents," your customers, your suppliers, your investors, and your team.

The Master Plan

A perfect example of the role of creativity would be the late Steve Jobs of Apple Computer. Although it could be argued that some of his tactics were less than completely admirable (read one of his biographies to see what I mean), I've seldom seen a leader who inspires such dedication in his team, or such admiration and loyalty from his customers. Mac people could be described as fanatics—not necessarily in a negative way—but who other than an Apple customer would line up outside an Apple Store hours before the release of a new iPhone or iPad? The phenomenon is largely due to Apple's unswerving devotion to creativity in everything they offer. Their products are beautifully designed, easy to use, and they perform as promised.

I admit I am no Steve Jobs, although there is one similarity between Apple and my company. Throngs of people get in line for Apple's latest offerings, but our investors line up in eager anticipation of our latest offerings, too. In fact, we used to send our proposals on new investments to our prospects via FedEx, but our investors on the West Coast complained that East Coast investors had a three-hour advantage, based on time zone differences, so our new programs would be sold out before people in California, Nevada, Oregon, and Washington had an opportunity to review the offers. (We have solved that issue by telling prospects in advance when new projects will be announced, and then announcing them via email so they all have an equal opportunity.)

I believe we have achieved success because, long before I ever heard of Steve Jobs, I took a look at successful individuals and companies and determined that they were successful because they focused on three key areas that gave them an edge. They are the components of an enduring Master Plan. They are:

1) People Power,

2) Product Power,

   and

3) Personal Power.

As you read this book, you may say to yourself, "These ideas are so simple, I could have thought of them." I'm sure you could have. What I believe makes this book significant and, hopefully, valuable to you, is the way these principles work together as a whole. In other words, as you begin to apply these principles to your life, your success in business and in life will be more meaningful to you.

I have discovered that there are no shortcuts to success. Success is a plan, and the creator of that plan—meaning you—has to work the plan.

Join me on a journey that is sure to bring a Master Plan to your life!

• • • • •

BACKGROUND

The question in the back of your mind—or maybe even in the front of your mind—right now may be, "Who is Mike Ingram and why should I care what he has to say?"

I think that's a valid question. When I read a book (and I read lots of them), I usually know something about the author, or about the person whose story is the focus of the book. I don't need to know anything about the author if my goal is to learn more about a specific subject. I love stories about the history of the Old West, so if a book comes highly recommended by people with the same interest, I don't care who the author is.

But in the case of this book, I am both the author and the subject. I am sharing my life with readers who know nothing about me.

So, why, then, should you care?

Before I answer that question, I want to make it very clear that I am not writing this book so that you will think I'm some "big deal." I am not the world's greatest anything. Not the world's greatest husband, father, or friend. Not the world's greatest boss or businessman. Not even the world's best example of the points I want to illustrate.

I am writing this book to give you a gift. That gift is my insight into what makes for a rewarding, fulfilling life. I'm here to say, "If you focus on these three simple principles in your daily life, there is no goal you can't reach. No dream you can't achieve."

I am proof of that, and that's why you should care.

My personal story is like most everyone else's. It's filled with ups and downs, successes and failures, joys and sorrows, and all the other things that become the complex mixture we call "our lives."

I am the product of a small-town upbringing. I worked several jobs throughout my years of junior high and high school. I went to college my freshman year at Pasadena Nazarene College (now known as Point Loma Nazarene University) in California. I went there because I was recruited for a swim team that never actually materialized. About the only thing I took seriously my freshman year was NHRA drag racing.

Then, a wonderful man, the dean of the college, Dean Paul Culbertson, called me into his office and strongly suggested I continue my education somewhere else and, based upon my aptitude testing, steered me towards a business degree. I decided then that I should probably get serious about my education, and I transferred to Texas Tech. Somewhere along the line, it dawned on me that people who had the better grade point averages were probably going to get better job offers and make more money.

I worked diligently to raise my lowly 2.0 GPA. I thoroughly applied myself the remainder of my years in college, and was named to the Alpha Zeta National Honor Fraternity (now Alpha Zeta Society), graduating from New Mexico University with a Bachelor of Science Degree in Agriculture in May, 1966.

My first job out of college was with America's Stores Packing Company in Pueblo, Colorado. I spent two years there and, during that time, my salary nearly doubled. But this was a meat packing plant, after all, and I really didn't enjoy the work. I decided to give sales a try, so I started representing Kirby vacuum cleaners. I'd begin my day at the packing plant at 5:00 a.m., then I'd go home, change clothes, and head out to sell Kirbys door-to-door, beginning at 5:00 p.m. I'd also sell on weekends.

Selling turned out to be one of my greatest skills, so eventually I took a job with Merck Pharmaceuticals in their animal health division. This position involved a move to Texas. After my first year, I was recognized as "Rookie of the Year," and I continued for four straight years as one of Merck's top producers.

While in my fourth year of employment, Merck had hired a man by the name of Dick White. Dick had previously been with 3M in a sales training position, and he is one of the most fantastic guys I've ever met in my life. He really opened my eyes to the basic essentials of selling. He introduced me to the "FAB" concept: how to present the <u>Features</u> of a product, the <u>Advantages</u> of that product, and the <u>Benefits</u> of the product.

He told me that most salespeople stop after talking about the Features and Advantages, but never really get to the Benefits—and it's the Benefits that the customers really want. It's the Benefits that close the sale. The Benefits are the personal reasons that people buy. Dick believed that to close a sale, a salesperson really needs to relate the purchase to a personal benefit of the product or service. (Zig Ziglar explains it this way: "People don't buy for logical reasons. They buy for emotional reasons.")

The concept of FAB was so simple, so true, and it clearly made sense to me. I adopted that philosophy—and I've used it ever since. Candidly, FAB is one of the most amazing things I've learned in my life. FAB should be a part of every salesperson's Master Plan.

Dick taught me many other valuable lessons about sales. He said, "The sales department isn't the whole company, but the whole company had better be the sales department." I've tried to apply that every day in every business in which I have been involved. No matter what business you undertake, even if you don't produce or sell any product, you are in the sales business. You are either selling product or you are selling service, one or the other, and THE WHOLE COMPANY HAD BETTER BE THE SALES DEPARTMENT.

As a result of applying what I had learned from Dick White, I was awarded several promotions, and I was given responsibility for conducting sales training meetings for distributors all over the county.

During my time with Merck, I realized that the sales reps were basically "representing" their products. They were educating the clientele—the veterinarians and the feedlots and the people in the animal health industry—but they were not asking for the order. They were detail people, not salespeople. In contrast, I was actually *writing* orders, which I then turned over to the wholesale distributors—Merck's customers. They, of course, loved that! The more Merck products they sold, the more I helped them, and the more we both prospered.

But a lot of the sales reps within the industry felt that asking for the order was beneath them and doing so would make them common salespeople. There were lots of company reps out there, including those from Pfizer, Eli Lily, and Upjohn. But I was one of the only reps out there writing a lot of orders every day and turning them in. I quickly earned a reputation within the industry.

The wholesale distributor salesmen realized that they needed to get close to me because of the business I was writing. Merck only sold through distributors; consequently, those distributors learned very quickly that I was going to support them if they were writing business for Merck products, and not for our competitors.

Because of my success at the very top of the sales charts, Merck tried to get me to move to the head office in New Jersey. In fact, they flew me there several times to interview for positions, but I had no interest in moving to the Eastern U.S. I have always loved the West too much to consider that.

In 1972, I left Merck to head up a new company, Tufts & Son of Oklahoma, Inc. This was loosely affiliated with Tufts & Son of Texas. The original company was founded by a wonderful friend and mentor, John Tufts, Sr. John was also in the animal health/pharmaceuticals industry, and he was interested in expanding his business into Oklahoma. John and I formed a partnership, and after putting up my farm as collateral for my part, I became half owner of an exciting new venture.

We started small. Initially, I was not only the President; I was also the only salesman. This suited me just fine, because I love sales. In fact, I gained the reputation as being the "Number One Rat Bait Salesperson in America." Yes, I said "rat bait." And, yes, I'll tell you more about that later!

Over time, we grew the company—which was eventually expanded into two other distribution companies: Western Vet and Sunwest Lawn and Garden—to a sales staff of 100, and more than $100 million in annual sales.

This success continued year after year—through lots of hard work and by surrounding myself with good people—until the energy companies in Texas and Oklahoma started experiencing a severe economic crisis. Oil was down from $40 per barrel to approximately $8 per barrel and, with that, oil companies were not renewing their mineral leases with landowners and farmers. This created a tremendous cash flow problem for many of my customers, as well as for local banks.

In a matter of two years, over 60 banks in Oklahoma alone went out of business. The bank with which I did business was taken over by the FDIC, and with rising receivables that were past due, my loans were called.

In trying to secure other bank financing from major banks on both coasts, I discovered that businesses in Oklahoma had been redlined and no banks were loaning to companies in that state.

I also discovered another shocking fact during this turbulent time: my "trusted" Chief Financial Officer had actually been embezzling from the company to the tune of several hundred thousand dollars. It was a crushing blow on a personal level, as well as financially. One of my longtime friends, Dr. Jim Little, offered financing, but rather than risk my friend's money, I ultimately sold out my companies and their divisions for pennies on the dollar.

The Master Plan

The sale created much-needed cash, but it also created a tax issue in several of my subsidiary corporations. My accountant strongly recommended bankrupting those corporations, but I found the idea of bankruptcy unacceptable for my situation and, instead, I chose to use the sale proceeds to pay the tax bills.

One of my mentors taught me a very valuable lesson that I employ daily as part of my Master Plan: "Friends come and go, but enemies accumulate." At this point in my life, it certainly seemed to me that I was in need of more friends.

Without a company and without any money, I moved my family—my wife Sheila and our six children— from Oklahoma to Phoenix, Arizona, to start over.

At that point, literally beginning from square one, there was no way that I could have ever dreamed what was about to unfold in my life. The decision to move my family to the "Valley of the Sun" was accompanied by my belief that I would someday be successful in real estate, but never would I have thought it possible that I would own ranches in three different states, including two ranches that John Wayne had owned for more than 40 years in Arizona—the Red River Ranch and the El Dorado Ranch.

Never did I dream that I would own some of the top quarter horses in the nation.

Never in a million years would I have envisioned that someday I would be a partner in a major league baseball team, the Arizona Diamondbacks—a "newbie" team that won the World Series against the New York Yankees in 2001.

But the most significant successes in my life have nothing to do with ranches, sports, or business. They are, instead, very personal.

Never did I imagine that I would one day be the proud father of six children, the delighted grandfather of twenty-one grandchildren, and the great-grandfather of eleven!

I admit that I did not do this on my own. Not only did I have a supportive partner, but I had the help of my good friend and mentor, Dr. James Dobson. My children were all raised under the guidelines of Dr. Dobson's book, *Dare to Discipline*, originally published in 1970 and updated in 1996 with *The New Dare to Discipline*.

As founder of Focus on the Family, Dr. Dobson's seven-part *Focus on the Family* series has been viewed by over 80 million people, and his radio program, *Family Talk*, a 30-minute daily broadcast, has a huge audience across the nation and around the world.

Granted, my kids have told me they still aren't overly fond of Dr. Dobson's strict principles, yet I'm glad I took his book to heart. I have learned so much from this great man and continue to learn from him today.

The opportunities and ultimate successes that came about as the result of the single decision to move to Arizona and start over have been astonishing… and the adventure continues from there! Please keep in mind that in writing this book I highlight my involvement; however, without my partners and team members working in concert with me, these accomplishments wouldn't have happened.

I hope the stories and lessons that I share in the following pages will engage you, inspire you, and empower you to create and follow your own master plan!

• • • • •

THE FIRST KEY: PEOPLE POWER

Chapter One
THE POWER OF RELATIONSHIPS

If you're like most people I've talked to, at some point in your life, a special person took you under his or her wing and became your mentor, your trusted advisor, your encourager, and your friend.

You may not have been looking for this person, you may not have expected this person to cross your path at the time and in the way it happened, and it may not have been until much later that you actually recognized the significant role this person had in your life. Because I don't know what to call these wonderful life surprises, I call them "Life's Greatest Gifts to Us."

My personal "Great Gift" is a man named Virgil Haley, a successful farmer from New Mexico. I had known him practically from birth, but I didn't really appreciate him until I was thirteen years old.

I grew up in Roswell, New Mexico. You know, the small town where some alien spacecraft supposedly crash-landed. I don't know if that's truth or fiction, because I never saw the crash site or any wreckage. And, I might add, I've never had contact with any extraterrestrial beings.

The Master Plan

My childhood was average in every way imaginable. My parents owned and operated a small 34-unit motel known as "the Navajo." They worked hard to keep the place clean and inviting, and to make every guest feel welcome.

Then, at the age of thirteen, the unimaginable happened and my "average" changed forever. My father died that year after battling cancer for three years, and my mom was left with a young son, an aging motel with a big mortgage, and a huge stack of medical and hospital bills. I had always helped out at the motel but, overnight, I became the man of the house and assistant keeper of the inn. With the bills piling up and the mortgage looming, there was no longer the luxury of having a large staff to help with the motel chores. In its place, just a very frightened widow and a thirteen-year-old kid.

The balance of my school years was spent getting up at a very early hour, cleaning what rooms I could before school, and continuing my work at the motel when I got home. I became the chambermaid, desk clerk, porter, switchboard operator, maintenance man (which included cleaning the never-ending parade of clogged toilets in the middle of the night), pool man, and snow removal expert. I learned at a very early age, if there's a job that has to be done, complaining about it doesn't get it done.

Every month as the mortgage payment came due, I worried that my mom wasn't going to be able to rent enough rooms to make it one more month. Summers were easier, as tourist traffic rolled through town, but winter months were very quiet.

I learned a bit about marketing, too—a subject I will discuss later. After sunset, I would go around the property and turn on the porch lights on every unit so if someone came, it wouldn't appear to be dark and unwelcoming.

During the summers, I was able to help out a little more with the finances. A local farmer, Virgil Haley, would pick me up late at night, and I would bale hay for him until sunup. I was paid $1 an hour…fairly good money back then! After working the fields, I would catch a couple hours of sleep and then head off to my other job as lifeguard at the local public swimming pool. Then, I'd get back to the motel for a little rest and some school homework at 1:00 p.m., before tourists started arriving around 4:00 or 5:00 p.m.

Throughout these years, it was Virgil who became my personal "Great Gift in Life." He was my friend, my encourager, and my employer—and, in many respects, he became a second father to me. Virgil had six sons of his own, so a lot of people in Roswell assumed I was his seventh son. That idea was reinforced when I would go to the store to pick up something for him and I'd sign for it with "Haley Farms" (with his permission, of course).

Not only was he able to give me a job and keep me gainfully employed, he would also take me hunting and fishing, he was the youth leader at my church, and he and his wife gave me hope and inspired me during difficult times. They instilled a lot of values in my life that are still core to my life principles today. Virgil is the guy who was always there for the teenagers, especially for *this* teenager. He gave, and gave, and gave… and I will forever be grateful to him.

I continued to work at the motel, as a lifeguard, and on Virgil's farm until I went away to college in 1962. Thankfully, my mother was able to pay off the mortgage on the Navajo in 1964, and she sold it and retired in 1979.

Take a moment and think back on your own life, about people you knew who were generous towards you and other people—and what an impact they had on your life. I still tell Virgil how much he means to me every time I have the opportunity.

But as important as Virgil is to me to this day, my mother, Maude Ingram, was a thousand times more important. I did my best to tell her how much I loved her and how she had impacted my life in endless wonderful ways… until that sad day in 2009 when she left our world. Now I wish I had told her every day.

Above all others, there is a very special person to whom I say, "I love you" every day. That's my wife Sheila. She's wonderful!

She always looks for the good in people—in every situation, she creates the model all of us should follow.

I am a believer in the institution of marriage… or, better yet, the joys of marriage. If you're not closer to your spouse than any other person, you're missing out on the best. Sheila and I aren't just husband and wife bound by a piece of paper. We're friends, mutual confidantes, involved parents, co-workers, and above all, spiritual partners. We travel together, socialize with friends together, laugh together, learn together, worship together, and pray together. Sheila blesses every day of my life!

Through Sheila, Virgil, and many others who came into my life, I have discovered the reasons why meaningful relationships are so important…and what it takes to make them work.

First, a healthy, meaningful relationship is open and honest. In this book, I discuss my thoughts on such topics as trust, integrity, and forgiveness. I see these as just some of the elements of an open and honest relationship.

Second, meaningful relationships are mutually supportive—truly a two-way street. This works in my marriage, because Sheila and I have shared values, so I know that she will support me, and she knows I will support her.

Third, relationships are the key to building the career you desire. One of the best examples I know of success through relationships is that of my friend, Red Steagall.

Red is a highly regarded Country-Western musician who got his start riding bulls in rodeos. Red celebrated his 80th birthday recently, and has spent his entire adulthood composing, performing, and promoting country music. Red has been awarded the Wrangler Award for original music five separate times and has composed, co-written, or performed with a number of country music legends including George Strait, Hank Snow, Nancy Sinatra, Glen Campbell, Toby Keith, Charley Pride, Charlie Daniels, and many others.

He discovered Reba McEntire while she was performing the national anthem at the National Rodeo Finals in Oklahoma City and signed her with Mercury Records. Ray Charles recorded Red's song "Here We Go Again" making it a hit, and it's been re-recorded sixty-three times by artists such as Nancy Sinatra, Johnny Duncan, and Roy Clark. Needless to say, there are other country music performers who have had more hits than Red; however, I do not believe any of them have had a greater impact and longevity in country music as Red. He has had over 200 of his compositions recorded both by him and by other artists. He has recorded 26 consecutive records that tracked on the national charts and has released a total of 22 albums.

Every year since 1991, Red has hosted "The Red Steagall Cowboy Gathering" in Fort Worth, which features a rodeo, country swing, country music and, poetry— drawing fans from across the nation, including numerous country music entertainers. Over the past 10 years, Red has additionally hosted a historic tour of the West, educating participants on the area selected, including the Code of the West, country music, and the meaning of specific lyrics.

In addition to being an accomplished composer and singer, Red has made numerous appearances on syndicated television shows including *Hee Haw* and *Nashville on the Road*. Since 1994, he has hosted a one-hour syndicated radio show, *Cowboy Corner*, hosted *In the Bunkhouse with Red Steagall* from 2010-2017 and now hosts *Red Steagall is Somewhere West of Wall Street* featuring stories and history of the West.

Some of Red's honors and awards include being named the Official Cowboy Poet Laurette of Texas, being presented with the Spirit of Texas award, and being inducted into the Texas Cowboy Hall of Fame, the Texas Trail of Fame, and the National Cowboy and Western Heritage Museum.

Recently, a group of businessmen has commissioned Bruce Greene, a renowned western artist to create a life-size statue of Red riding on his horse. This statue was placed on the east lawn of the Cowtown Coliseum in Fort Worth to celebrate the 29th year of the

Red Steagall Cowboy Gathering by honoring the man who started it all.as well as to remind everyone of his contribution to western heritage for years to come.

Red freely admits that he has built his entertainment career on the foundation of diverse relationships. One of those relationships is with me; Red is not only a friend but also a partner in El Dorado investment properties.

Red also introduced me to Johnny Trotter of Hereford, Texas. Owing to his many relationships, Johnny is successful in every business venture he undertakes. He does many of his deals on the basis of a simple handshake, because he is honest, trustworthy, and follows through on his commitments.

Johnny sits on the boards of several banks and is President of one of the largest cattle feeding operations in the nation, as well as a large Ford dealership in Hereford. He also owns ranches in Texas, New Mexico, Oklahoma, and Mississippi. Even though Johnny is extremely busy with his numerous business enterprises, he's given his valuable time and experience to the American Quarter Horse Association, serving as past President, Director, and a member of their Executive Committee. As a life-time member of this great association, I value his contributions and his continued commitment. Johnny's commitment to relationships makes people want to seek him out and be a part of whatever he does.

The Master Plan

I was so honored to co-introduce him, along with Red Steagall, when Johnny was presented with the Chester A. Reynolds Memorial Award at the National Cowboy & Western Heritage annual event March, 2018. The award is named after the Museum's founder and awarded to an individual for unwavering commitment to the future of the American West. No one is more deserving of this award than Johnny.

In my introduction of Johnny as he received this award in Oklahoma City, I began by saying "Anyone could have found success if they had the inheritance that he received." Yes, you would think he came into a lot of money, but no, it was something much better. He was born the son of a Methodist preacher who was pastor with Johnny's mother. You could find Johnny on the front row at that small Texas town church each and every Sunday.

He was taught it was better to give than to receive. He was taught the Ten Commandments, the Golden Rule, and to love others as yourself. His word is his bond. His name stands for integrity. Johnny's inheritance was so much greater than any amount of money. He received the right foundation for success. His mother was sitting at the front table that night and was beaming with pride with tears in her eyes.

Johnny's latest venture, along with three other businessmen, is the purchase of the Ruidoso Downs Race Track, home to the nation's richest quarter horse race held each year on Labor Day in the White Mountains of New Mexico. One of Johnny's first improvements after the purchase was the construction of a new chapel at the track for the use of the owners, trainers, jockeys, and visitors.

I was happy to welcome him into his first investment with El Dorado several years ago, and I hope to partner with him for years to come.

The bottom line to all of this is that I discovered from my mother and from Virgil—and from others in the intervening years, and especially from Sheila—that there is power in relationships. Value them. Nurture them. And give back in every way you can. They are a vital part of your master plan.

• • • • •

Chapter Two
THE POWER OF NETWORKING

There's an old axiom that seems to apply to both business and to life: "It's not WHAT you know; it's WHO you know."

While I definitely believe in acquiring knowledge AND wisdom, it's not so much what I've learned that has built my ventures. It's the people who have come into my life. This, of course, reconnects with the whole idea of relationships.

I had two great friends in the area of networking—Ted Purdy, a 19-year PGA golf professional, and Ed Hackey, an insurance guru. Both of these gentlemen are pros at networking and have introduced me to so many great people over the years, I will be eternally grateful. Not only are they two of the greatest people I've ever met, the people they know and have introduced me to are of the same caliber.

A great story of networking comes from my friend, Harvey Mackay. Starting early in life, Harvey held many jobs, including selling magazines door-to-door, newspaper delivery boy, snow removal expert (with a shovel), and lawn mower. When Harvey graduated college, he became an envelope salesman for Quality Park Envelope Company. At the same time, he also joined Minneapolis' Oak Ridge Country Club to play golf—but mainly to network with all of the area businessmen. This networking led to Harvey becoming Quality Park's top salesman. Five years later, he used those proceeds to purchase an insolvent envelope company that he grew into a multi-million dollar company. He sold that company in 2000, while remaining an equal partner and Chairman. Harvey went on to become a very successful writer and international speaker. His first book, *Swim with the Sharks without Being Eaten Alive*, was on the New York Times bestseller list for 54 weeks and has sold more than 5 million copies. It was followed by several other additional bestsellers. In 2004, Harvey was inducted into Horatio Alger Association. Harvey is one of those people who just brightens up any room he enters and one of the best networkers I've ever had the pleasure to know.

    I believe in opening my mind and heart to all sorts of relationships. Many times over the years, the people in my life have told me that my ability to find common ground in relationships is my most intriguing quality. I believe that it is this aptitude that has enabled me to accomplish some very difficult endeavors in my life, from getting a road built and designated as a state highway, to obtaining zoning changes that everyone else said could not be done. I have found that if I can get a group of people to concentrate and focus on their commonalities rather than their differences, I can accomplish all sorts of things. Amazing things!

I can tell you that I have built long-lasting relationships with people of many different nationalities and faiths. Some of my best friends are Native Americans, and I cherish these friendships and those with people of many other ethnic origins.

I have also worked hard to develop relationships with people of different political views. I have great friends who are Democrats, Republicans, and Independents. True, there are times that you may never get individuals of different beliefs to agree; however, they may find that they are closer to agreement than they originally believed if you can build a relationship.

Among my good friends who express very different political views than mine are Tom Brokaw and Brian Greenspun. Tom, of course, is one of the world's best-known news anchors. He is the only person to have hosted all of the major NBC news shows including *The Today Show*, *NBC Nightly News* and *Meet the Press*. He is also the author of the wonderful book, *THE GREATEST GENERATION*.

Brian is the developer of the very successful Green Valley master-planned development in Henderson, Nevada, and also the President and Publisher of *THE LAS VEGAS SUN*.

I thoroughly enjoy any time I am able to spend with these two good men; however, when we are together, we concentrate on things we have in common rather than areas of disagreement.

I've known these gentlemen both for a number of years, and we've simply agreed to disagree. We discuss our opinions but always leave as friends. I can't believe I've not been able to convince them of my views, and I am very sure they both feel the same.

The significance of building relationships is something I discovered very early in my life. It is the first step in unleashing the power of networking.

I believe there are four ways in which we network:

1) Other people come to us—with their vision, their specific ideas, their connections (relationships), and their opportunities.
2) We go to other people—with our vision, our ideas, our connections, and our opportunities.
3) Other people (or situations) connect us. This can be the result of the recommendations of satisfied clients, or through various types of "lead groups."
4) God "does His thing." You may not believe in God, so you might prefer to call this "fate," or "chance," or the "law of the universe," or something else. I can simply tell you that I've seen and experienced too many things in my life that I could not satisfactorily explain apart from God. You can accept or reject that as you choose, of course.

I moved my family to Phoenix, Arizona, in 1986. But many things happened in my life before that day—some of them frightening, some of them enlightening, but most of them amazing. For a moment, let me take you a little deeper into my history so I may share with you some of the more extraordinary moments in my life.

First, after I resigned from Merck, I left Colorado in my rearview mirror in 1972 and relocated to Oklahoma City, Oklahoma, where I built a successful career and three separate businesses selling veterinary medicines to farmers, ranchers, farm stores, and veterinarians. This later expanded in 1974 to include a new subsidiary, Sunwest Lawn and Garden. Homer Lacky, the former Pfizer representative, took the lead and built the company into one of the largest distribution companies in that field in the nation. I later sold this business to a division of Weyerhauser in 1984. Jim Graber, the leading salesperson at Diamond Labs, and Jim Keller, the president at Abbot Labs, both joined in our venture. In 1978, we formed another subsidiary known as Western Veterinarian Supply, which sold products exclusively to veterinarians.

As I mentioned earlier, things turned from great to awful during the oil crisis of the 1980s. Banks in Oklahoma and Texas were failing in alarming numbers. Worse yet, no banks outside those two major oil states would make loans to Oklahoma or Texas companies… no matter what the industry. I wanted to grow my company, but Oklahoma had been "redlined." I went to the East Coast, I went to the West Coast. No one would replace my line of credit.

To keep my family going, I was considering a job in Dallas. Sheila was not at all fond of the idea of moving to Texas. Her roots were in Oklahoma City—her entire family lived there. Plus, she thought it would be hard on the kids if we uprooted them. But she ultimately accepted the idea.

Then, along came an interesting suggestion from a master networker named Bill Burch. Bill insisted that I not sign a new contract to move to Dallas. Instead, he invited me to visit him in Arizona. I traveled with Bill down to Tucson for a meeting and had the opportunity to meet wonderful business people from both Phoenix and Tucson. Being a history buff, I was excited on our way back to Phoenix to see Picacho Peak, where the Western-most battle of the Civil War took place.

That night, we were sitting in his hot tub in the backyard of his home, looking up through the palm trees at the moon and I said, "This is about as close to heaven as I think I could be." It happened to be February 9th, a perfect winter night in Arizona.

When I got out of the hot tub, I called home to check in with Sheila. I asked, "How is everything in Oklahoma City?"

She replied, "Well, we didn't have school today. There was a huge ice storm, so school was cancelled."

I thought that was a perfect time to introduce an entirely new concept, so I said, "Sheila, we're moving to Arizona."

She immediately started crying. She had already done her level best to accept the fact that we were going to move to Dallas, which was three hours away from three of our six kids who were already enrolled in college, and her three sisters and her mom and her dad, whom she'd never been away from in her life. Now I had upset the apple cart once again.

I said, "Sheila, you're going to love Arizona."

She wasn't sure about that at all… and told me so. Two weeks later I brought them out during spring break to see Arizona. Sheila absolutely cried throughout the entire trip. Her eyes were almost swollen shut by the time we hit Phoenix.

I thought I had planned a great sales strategy by bringing them down to Phoenix through Sedona and its Red Rocks—the stunning beauty of Arizona.

But it was when we arrived in Phoenix and our kids saw all the palm trees and the green grass that the tide turned. You have to realize that this was March and there was not a lot of green grass in Oklahoma in March. They said, "Oh wow, Dad, this is really cool!"

Sheila turned around and said, "Shut up, kids."

Sheila was not impressed with Arizona at all. She still did not want to leave Oklahoma, but I felt strongly that it was the right business decision that would allow me to provide for my family. I went ahead and moved out to Arizona alone the next month. I wanted to begin fresh and operate my own business. The idea of working for someone else in Dallas after having owned my own business simply didn't appeal to me.

A few weeks later, Sheila and my mother-in-law reluctantly loaded a U-Haul truck back in Oklahoma and drove it to Arizona.

Thanks to Bill Burch's networking efforts, we got off to a fast start in our new city. Bill immediately found ways to introduce me to people I never imagined I'd know. In 1987, I co-founded a company that still exists today—El Dorado Holdings, Inc.

The mission of our company was (and still is) to buy desert land that some would say is worthless and transform it into something significant. To do this, we needed to find investors who could capture our vision and believe in the future. I had no money—for reasons I introduced in the Background chapter. So I needed OPM—"Other People's Money."

Naturally, some of our very first investors were people Bill Burch introduced us to in Arizona, as well as friends and business associates in Oklahoma. Bill personally invested $8,000 of his hard-earned money with us in 1992. Because he was placing his faith and trust in my idea that money could be made on worthless desert land, I had to prove to him and my investors that I could help them get what they wanted—namely a return on their investment.

My good friend, the late Zig Ziglar, often said, "You can get everything in life you want if you help enough other people get what they want." I have demonstrated that those words are true.

This ties in with networking. If you're helping other people get what they want, you will become a part of their networks, and they will bring you more new relationships and more business than you could possibly imagine.

You can build a business on networking. And it can become loyal, repeat business. Many of the people to whom Bill Burch introduced me 20 or 25 years ago are still investors. Many of them have participated in every investment I have ever offered.

I'm obviously not going to tell you how much money they've made by investing in my projects, but one of them recently told me, "I've never done as well on any of my other investments." In fact, Bill Burch himself paid a visit to our office in late 2017. He asked, "How much money have I made with my investments in El Dorado Holdings?" We did the calculations, and replied, "Your initial investment of $8,000 and your reinvestments have generated over $1.6 million in distributions (approximately $900,000 in profits) and your remaining property assets are valued at around

$900,000+." He was elated and wanted to know when the next investment opportunity would be available. Networking prepares fruitful business relationships, just as tilling and fertilizer prepare good soil for a future harvest.

At this point, you might be thinking to yourself, "Mike just uses his networks to make more money. He's part of the reason for the 'Occupy Wall Street" movement. (Or whatever it's called at the time you read these words.)

You can choose to believe or not believe in what I say, but, for me, life is not all about money. But money can accomplish a lot of good, when used in the right ways. I seek to do exactly that.

Today, my personal goal is not simply to build a business through networking, but to help create value in other people's lives. By that, I mean I want to help them with their passions and support their charities of choice. Yes, they have to be charities that are compatible with my personal beliefs and my desire to help others. But I'm not narrow minded about it. If people are truly helped— and the charities are not pointlessly enriched—I can usually get behind them.

Ultimately, I believe that networking is a two-way street. It's not two-way if you use networking only to your benefit. Many times, my sole benefit from networking is helping the other person. I believe that if you help someone, they in turn, will be much more likely to help someone else. I know, in my life, the people that have helped me along the way have certainly empowered me to help others.

If you see the power of networking as something you want to work only on your behalf, you won't enjoy the benefits that come from the giving side of the equation.

I learned this from Bill Burch. I continue to apply what I have learned from Zig Ziglar. This lesson has proven much more valuable to me than any lesson I learned in school.

People are important. To get what you want out of life, help them get what *they* want. It all starts with relationships, and then it is built upon networking.

• • • • •

Chapter Three

THE POWER OF PARTNERSHIPS

Life is better when you have partners with whom you share ideas, enjoy events, and build businesses.

Yet, many people in today's world are skeptical of partnerships. That's because they've seen partnerships fail. They've watched as marriages have failed and torn families apart. They've seen businesses fail when business partners have gone at each other's throats.

I believe there is a way to build a partnership that will last. I call it "The Common Good."

In a truly "working" partnership:

1) There is a shared goal—the pursuit of a shared outcome;
2) Everyone is an equal: even if their investments aren't exactly the same, the payoff is based fairly on the investor's proportionate share;
3) When one wins, all win;
4) When one loses, all lose (sad, but true);
5) One success logically leads to future successes… but if there is a loss, we learn from it and move forward.

RICHARD CHILDRESS

I recently had an interesting conversation with a good friend, Richard Childress. You may know his name, because he has been involved in NASCAR for many years, founding Richard Childress Racing (RCR) in 1969. In fact, Richard currently has nine racing teams on the circuit. He has more than 200 victories across NASCAR'S top three series and 17 championships. He is the first in NASCAR'S history to win championships in all three national touring series. His team has racked up three Daytona 500 wins (including one in 2018), as well as three Brickyard 400 victories.

Richard is one of the top three names in racing today and in 2017 was inducted into the NASCAR Hall of Fame.

In addition to his success in racing, Richard is also a long-time member of the Sportsmen's Foundation and the National Rifle Association and established the Childress Institute for Pediatric Trauma. Its purpose is to discover and share the best ways to prevent and treat severe injuries in children.

Before I tell you about Richard's success in partnerships in his business, I must tell you about his most successful partnership, and that is with his wife, Judy. That partnership is the strongest by far. Judy and I agree on many things, but the one point we strongly agree on, and is engraved on a plaque on her desk. "Whatever women do they must do twice as well as men to be thought half as good. Luckily, this is not difficult." (Quote by Charlotte Whitton)

Richard Childress has assembled a team of dedicated partners. He has team members who have been with him for more than 30 years. They have one shared goal—winning races. He finds investors and sponsors who have a vested interest in that outcome. They all know that they will be faced with both wins and losses. But losses do not deter them from their goal of always pursuing the win. They learn from losses and move on. After Richard retired from active driving, his eldest grandson, Austin Dillon, took over his flagship car in 2014. Austin won the most coveted race, The Daytona 500, in 2018, winning that exciting race in overtime. Richard's other grandson, Ty, is now also part of the RCR team.

Richard's principles for building successful partnerships are actually very simple:

- Have a clear dream;
- Find and empower great people;
- Become unified in the pursuit of that dream.

That's the power of partnerships!

Here's how it works at our company, El Dorado Holdings.

Back before El Dorado existed, I occasionally invested in other people's business opportunities, but they were limited partnerships. In limited partnerships, the general partner had all the power and the limited partners had none. They were also usually structured with substantial upfront and ongoing fees to the general partner. It only took a couple of these ventures for me to determine that they were not for me.

When I started El Dorado, I wanted my investors to be partners with me. I didn't just want their money; I sought their input and wanted them to feel like they were a part of the deal, and not just sitting on the outskirts waiting for something to happen. I began structuring El Dorado's investments as general partnerships, but then converted them to limited liability companies when that structure became available in Arizona. Every time we create a new opportunity for an investment in land or buildings, we set up a Limited Liability Company—an LLC. I remain averse to bank lending except for some of our income producing properties and prefer to raise cash for all other investment opportunities.

In Arizona and many other states, LLCs can be set up in one of two ways. They can either be "manager-managed" or they can be "member-managed." In El Dorado's LLCs, I, and all other investors, are members. Our LLCs are "member-managed," and El Dorado is only the day-to-day manager. El Dorado is subject to the members' will. That means that the other members—the other investors—can get together at any time and decide by majority vote to fire me.

That also means that the members decide when and at what price to sell, or even not to sell. All major decisions are made as a group, and our team works diligently to make sure that all members are kept informed of activity including local, regional, and even national news that could affect their particular investment.

Even though I am the one who initially established the LLC, I have to perform. I have to do my job. People often ask me, "Mike, how do you protect yourself?" The answer is always the same; I make sure the members are pleased with my performance.

In successful partnerships, those who have the responsibility to perform do exactly that. To date, El Dorado has formed over 130 LLCs that include over 83,000 acres of land. We have entitled and/or developed close to 50,000 residential lots, several thousand acres of commercial/retail property and several golf courses. In addition, we have owned and managed approximately 250,000 square feet of office space and over 1,300 apartment units. All of these ventures are LLCs controlled by our investors—our partners.

In the same sense, employees can and should become your partners in your business. In fact, I don't even like the word "employee;" I prefer "team member." In the ideal situation, the employer and the team member become partners in the sense that they have shared goals and shared responsibilities for a successful outcome.

I think about the people I've been fortunate enough to work with over the years. For many years now, my valued right-hand "assistant" has been Denise Organ. She's not only a loyal team member, she's family to Sheila and me. Her husband, Scott, and her kids are all family. In my 48+ years in business and many executive assistants throughout, I can honestly state that no one comes close to Denise. She has an uncanny ability to know what needs to be done far before I do and is always one step ahead. I know my very busy schedule and travel would be a challenge to most anyone, but Denise handles it all with professionalism and tact. Her judgement and diplomacy when handling difficult situations are unparalleled. I would truly be lost without her so I try to make sure she is happy in her position and never leaves.

Then, as I walk around our office and see the people who work here today, I feel that each and every one of them are family members. I've told them that when they came to work at El Dorado, they should tear up their resumes because they will never look for another job.

Even in downturns—in a terrible real estate recession like the one we went through in recent years—we've not had to lay off one team member. I'm so thankful for that. We really do need one another to build our future together.

My experience with successful partnerships goes back to my association with John Tufts, years ago, when I lived in Oklahoma City. I had been working with Merck Pharmaceuticals for several years, and had built a very successful career as one of their top reps.

But John Tufts, Sr. entered my life and provided an opportunity for me to become a partner in Tufts & Son of Oklahoma. My task was to open up a new distributorship that represented more than 300 companies, primarily in Oklahoma.

In 1980, I brought in my best friend in life, Roy McKay, president of McKay Oil Company, as an investor so that we could expand into additional states. Eventually, that company and its subsidiaries expanded into five other states.

In 1985, I moved to Arizona and eventually founded El Dorado Holdings, Inc., with Monty Ortman. We had both moved to Arizona at about the same time, and we were introduced by a mutual friend. We were both essentially starting over in our lives, so it was a good match. For 23 years, we had one of the greatest partnerships that I've ever seen. When Monty called me one day and said he wanted to spend more time with his kids and grandkids, I agreed to buy his share of our partnership. Our partnership may have been over but our friendship continued.

These partnerships are successful because the partners all seek the Common Good.

There are other people who built their businesses through relationships with big corporations and big investment funds. But I don't really think of those arrangements as real relationships.

I've chosen to build my business through partnerships with other entrepreneurial business people. And these partnerships turn into real relationships. We fish together, we hunt together, and we travel together. In a very real sense, I am a part of their family, and they're a part of my family. They actually stay at my house when visiting Phoenix.

I have investors today who have a key to my home in Phoenix, and know they are welcome to simply "check themselves in" to our guest house. They feel comfortable enough to stay at our house whether we are home or not. They are welcome to fly into Phoenix, rent a car, and go to the house. It's been that way for more than 30 years. After all, my investors are my partners and my family.

There should be no doubt in your mind that there is power in partnerships. To make them work, you have to invest your time and keep the idea of Common Good in mind at all times.

Good things in life generally do not happen by accident. Successful partnerships are usually the result of attention and intention.

· · · · ·

Chapter Four
THE POWER OF TEAMWORK

Have you ever met someone who thought they could do it all themselves? They didn't need anyone. They could achieve all of their goals on their own.

I imagine there are some "go it alone" people who don't need the involvement of others in their lives, but I've never personally met any of them. Working with a team toward a specific goal or outcome can be one of the most rewarding experiences any of us can have. I mentioned Richard Childress of NASCAR fame, and he is clear proof of that.

For this discussion, I'm going to assume that you don't need to be sold on the value of teamwork. Rather, I'm going to offer my thoughts on the attributes of a good team player. I've always looked for four qualities:

- A Winner's Attitude.

- A Strong Work Ethic.

- Uncompromising Character.

- The Ability to Forgive and Reconcile.

Let's look at them one at a time.

A WINNER'S ATTITUDE

As far as I'm concerned, the only attitude a real winner can have and display is a positive one.

Everyone who is a part of my team today has the attitude of a winner. One of my favorite Zig Ziglar quotes is, "Your attitude, not your aptitude, will determine your altitude."

People who exude positive attitudes will "fly higher" than those who don't. That's why, if I have a choice, I will associate with people who find the good in life's experiences, rather than the bad. For me, this is not only a personal matter—it extends to my work relationships.

I recall a wonderful young woman who was at our reception desk for many years. She was very candid with me: she wanted to move from the front desk to another area that she thought would offer increased responsibility and greater opportunity.

I didn't want to hold her back, but I still kept challenging her to stay in her position. I said, "You will be the highest paid front desk person in this town if you just realize how important you are in your position. You have a winner's attitude, and the first time people walk through our door, they realize that."

Finally, she realized that she was making a great contribution to our company—because her talents, her people skills, her telephone voice, and the ways she greeted people were so important. Ultimately, we gave her additional responsibilities in office administration. Everyone realized she was the one in charge of so many things; much more than answering the phone, greeting people, and getting them coffee.

In fact, I think the receptionist position is one of the hardest roles to fill because that person is the very first representation of your company. Dr. Ken Blanchard, the globally recognized business author and consultant, calls that position the "Director of First Impressions." That title actually appears on a sign at the reception desk at The Ken Blanchard Companies. I think I am going to borrow that idea because this position is so valuable.

A few years ago, my long-time Director of First Impressions decided she wanted to be a stay-at-home mom and raise a family. She still continues to work on projects from home (I don't give up on talent easily), but I honestly thought I would never be able to replace her.

Thankfully, "Efficient Karen" walked into our lives at El Dorado, and she has become yet another perfect "Director of First Impressions." I intend to make sure that our Ms. Mickalonis (Karen) remains happy and challenged, because I know what an important job she has and how difficult it can be to find that special person who makes the right first impression.

A STRONG WORK ETHIC

People often ask me why I work so hard. There are two reasons for my dedication to work.

First, I have a responsibility toward my investors. If it were only my money involved in all our projects, I wouldn't work nearly as hard, I guarantee you. But when others invest their money and trust in me, it naturally puts me in a different place—where I must do my very best.

Second, I like the financial rewards…because I can continue to give generously to organizations in which I believe. To quote Zig again, "I've been with money and without it…and it's better with it."

My philosophy is very simple: Work Hard and Play Hard. I believe that the people who are on my team understand this about me, and they, too, are willing to work hard for the rewards they receive.

Right now, I'm thinking about Deb Bricker, one of the smartest and most loyal and dedicated people I've ever encountered. I value her as a partner, a team member, and a trusted friend. Deb has been with El Dorado Holdings exactly one day less than I have. That's since 1987. In fact, Deb has capably served us as a director, my partner, and our "Designated Broker," a position that is required within every company working in the field of real estate. I always love to tell the story that our partners used to call and ask to speak to me about their investments until they figured out I would have to ask Deb. Over the years, partners have learned to go directly to Deb to find out the status and our plans on their investments. She is the over-viewer of all that is El Dorado. I am always reminded of the saying, "Do you want to speak to the man in charge or the woman who knows what's going on?'

Ms. Bricker—and the rest of the great people who are on the team—will come in early and stay late because they have solid work ethics. They understand the importance of:

- Getting the job done;
- Doing the job right;

   and

- Meeting or exceeding the customer's expectations.

When the people on my team take on an assignment, they are promising me that they'll finish it. However, the world is full of people who can finish the job. I look for the ones who tend to the small details.

My team also gives everything they've got to do the job right. "Whatever it takes" could be their mantra. They realize that customers have legitimate expectations that must be met—or those customers will soon become ex-customers.

This all comes down to work ethic, and it's an individual trait that people either possess or they don't. I look for the people who do.

While a college degree usually indicates that an individual possesses a certain degree of dedication and focus, when I'm hiring, I don't look too much at an individual's educational experience; I look at his or her desire to excel. That desire is a key component of work ethic. I believe hard work and perseverance will usually outweigh a truckload of book smarts.

Evidence seems to show that this trait is instilled at a very early age. For example, I need to point out that my associate of so many years, Deb Bricker, has a very strong work ethic. In the course of her full-time career with us, she also raised two kids into two exceptional adults. Deb spent a lot of her career in the oil fields of Wyoming. Her mom and dad were very hard workers. It "ran in the family," because Deb's sister (who sadly passed away at far too young an age), was also very intelligent and had a strong work ethic. I suspect that trait was taught and modeled in the home.

UNCOMPROMISING CHARACTER

I've never found a written or oral exam that can help me determine a person's character, yet character is another important thing I seek in a team member.

I always sit down with prospects and engage in conversation about their background, because the past tells a lot about the future. In my mind, I ask, "Will the people I'm doing business with—whether it's clients or partners—look at this person and have respect for him or her and realize that this is a person of high integrity?"

This is so important, because any person you hire is going to be representing you and your values. After I've talked with candidates for a while, I start getting a sense… a gut feeling… about their values and what's really important to them. Is it more than just a paycheck?

I've also been able to recognize the innate qualities of people in other positions with other companies. If someone has obvious character in another job, it's certainly going to carry over to the new position. For example, I knew Jim Kenny, Linda Cheney, Brad Hinton, and Chris Grogan all through other firms where I had watched them perform. I had a history with them. I watched Jim Kenny, the president of our company today, as he came up through three other companies with which I had enjoyed relationships. He had accepted and welcomed greater responsibility with each of these companies.

Here's a little secret tactic I use when I'm looking for new team members, I often will seek out people who aren't looking for a change. When I hired Jim Kenny, he wasn't looking for a job. I went to him. Since taking over as El Dorado's president, Jim has been highly sought after to participate in numerous real estate and economic development organizations. He is a member of Greater Phoenix Leadership, Maricopa Association of Governments, Canada Arizona Business Council and I-11 Coalition. In addition, he sits on the Board of Directors of WESTMARC, as well as the Arizona Chamber of Commerce, the Valley Partnership and the Maricopa Economic Development Alliance. Jim's expertise is very valuable to these organizations and, in turn, his participation provides El Dorado a "seat at the table" to promote and protect our investments.

Likewise, our Senior Vice President, Linda Cheney, was not looking for change. I went to her and presented the opportunity to join El Dorado. Linda's background in engineering and her eye for detail add an extremely valuable component to our team. Like Jim, Linda represents El Dorado in area organizations important to our landholdings, including the Maricopa Stanfield Irrigation and Drainage District and the Pinal Partnership (she's a Board Member) and a member of Valley Partnership, the Lower Santa Cruz River Alliance, and the Homebuilders Association of Central Arizona. Her experience has been so valuable to the City of Maricopa, I've been told several times by City and County administrators she should be on their payroll due to her contributions.

Brad Hinton, our Director of Planning and Development, had previously worked in the planning department for the City of

Maricopa, an office we deal with frequently due to our many real estate projects there. He then moved on to a large homebuilding firm. I am so pleased Brad is now working as a trusted El Dorado team member and he's playing an essential role in planning and developing our major investment properties in Maricopa and elsewhere. I knew all of these people and the standards they held high because I had observed them.

El Dorado's accounting office is made up of two women of utmost integrity whose opposite personalities harmonize with each other. Our long-time controller, Janet Stewart, is a fairly serious, unshakable "watcher of the funds," and still takes on numerous special El Dorado assignments, even though she is semi-retired. We were extremely fortunate to find Al Blasi to take over for Janet several years ago, and I couldn't be more pleased with how Al has fit into our organization. Our bookkeeper, Louise Leland, is a bubbly soul whose delightful laugh can often be heard throughout our office. Just hearing her laugh makes everyone else smile. That is why she has been designated "Director of Humor."

A newer key member of our ever-evolving team is Stephanie Morrison, who heads up the Investor Relations Department and works directly with Deb Bricker to interact with all of our partners and keep them informed of their various investments. She has also stepped into the role of Associate Broker for our company.

Though she didn't know it when she started, she has a talent for the business aspects of raising and training registered quarter horses. What a bonus for me! I love those horses.

Since I am always in the market for talent, even in rough economic times, back in 2012, I added a young man named Chris Grogan to our team. Chris had a successful real estate career at CB Richard Ellis, but I saw attributes in Chris that would complement El Dorado, so I convinced Chris to make a change.

Upon his hiring, I immediately determined that Chris could logically become the "face of El Dorado" in business negotiations and also at events and conventions. Every company that wants to survive long-term must add competent, engaged people who can carry forward into the future. His fictitious title is "Event Planner Extraordinaire," due to his fantastic ability to plan and coordinate investor events, such as an investor gathering we hosted in Washington, D.C. That meeting included a tour of the "Museum of the Bible," a remarkable facility funded by David and Barbara Green, founders of Hobby Lobby.

Chris is also deeply involved in our relationships with our investors along with searching out new investment opportunities and marketing our established properties. Due to his ability and hard work since he joined El Dorado, I'm proud to add Chris as an El Dorado partner, joining Deb and Jim in that position. Naturally,

I'm looking forward to watching him grow and reach his full potential at El Dorado.

THE ABILITY TO FORGIVE AND RECONCILE

I know you may not believe me when I tell you this, but I honestly cannot recall a single instance in which someone on our team has spoken an unkind, angry word to another team member. Yes, we have our discussions—our disagreements—but they do not escalate to anything more. It might be that I am simply blessed to find amazing people with cooperative spirits!

Yet, at some point, every team is going to experience some sort of conflict… and sometimes it won't be pretty. That's where the ability to forgive and reconcile comes into play.

I'm going to discuss forgiveness in more detail in Part Three of the book: Personal Power. But for now, I want to emphasize the simple truth that, in a fast-paced, highly competitive business environment, people sometimes disagree, and sometimes tempers can flare. A true team player will be able to forgive any wrongs—for the good of the organization—and reconcile as quickly as possible. It takes maturity, personal strength, and positive self-esteem to forgive and move on.

When you look at the four characteristics of effective team members—A Winner's Attitude, A Strong Work Ethic,

Uncompromising Character, and The Ability to Forgive and Reconcile—it all comes down to one thing: *It's a matter of the heart!*

• • • • •

Chapter Five

THE POWER OF LOYALTY

Some of the greatest illustrations of loyalty—as well as the *lack* of loyalty—can be found in literature as well as throughout history. There are endless recorded stories of the betrayal of leaders—both the respected ones as well as the "not-so-worthy."

The point simply is, I believe that if you want to build loyalty among your followers—your team—you have to be a leader worth following.

You may think that the following points are far too simple and obvious—that you've heard them, seen them, or read them before. That everyone reading this book already knows and applies them.

I wish that were true. But I meet leaders all the time who overlook—even forget—many of the basics. In order to gain the loyalty of your team, these are the five most vital habits you must nurture in your personal and business life:

1) BE TRANSPARENT ABOUT WHO YOU ARE. Very simply, no one will be loyal to a phony. Leaders who admit their shortcomings not only gain respect, but they attract followers who can help them "fill in the blanks." I've always told Sheila, "Please don't ever let me become arrogant." She is very good at reminding me… she could keep anyone humble!

2) MAKE YOUR VISION CLEAR. Most leaders have a vision for their lives and organizations. But I'm amazed by how many leaders are unable to articulate that vision. I believe in telling the team—then telling them again, then reminding them continuously—what my vision is. Understanding is the first step to "buying in," and you need the buy-in of everyone on your team to follow the path you set forth.

3) CLARIFY YOUR SPECIFIC GOALS. You understand that realizing a vision is an ongoing process. Smaller, easily defined goals are part of that process. My team and I had a vision for creating a new city in the middle of the desert south of Phoenix. It actually came about—the process will be described later in this book. But it was the methodical achievement of small, incremental goals that led to the big picture—the vision that became Maricopa, Arizona. As Zig Ziglar has wisely pointed out, "A goal properly set is halfway reached."

4) MEASURE PROGRESS TOWARD THOSE GOALS. It's been said, "Without a plan and a deadline, a goal is really nothing more than a dream." That's why I believe that every goal needs a deadline, no matter how small the goal may seem to be. By checking both big and little things off the list, you can get a better sense of your

progress. Very few people I have ever met can see the entire outline of their goal at the beginning. As Zig Ziglar explained to me many years ago, "If you can't see the entire plan, go as far as you can see. When you reach that point, I can guarantee you, you will be able to see further." Sometimes along the way, you may need to make slight adjustments to your path, but that does not mean that you abandon your ultimate goal. Zig also said that some people are a wandering generality… having a good time… whatever makes them feel good. It's better to be a meaningful specific, someone with a goal. Make a difference, or as Paul Harvey used to say, "Leave the wood pile higher than you found it."

5) ACKNOWLEDGE AND REWARD SUCCESS. Nothing discourages a team member more quickly and thoroughly than lack of appreciation on the part of the leader. And discouragement destroys loyalty. There are many ways to acknowledge and reward success, but the two ways that most team members appreciate are praise and pay increases or bonuses. When someone is both privately and publicly praised, and when that praise is followed by a monetary reward, there should be no doubt that the team member's contributions were valued.

Depending on the business venture I'm involved in, I actively seek and nurture the loyalty of four groups: Employees (or Team Members), Suppliers, Investors, and Customers. In the sales and distribution business, I naturally worked with suppliers and manufacturers, while in the land development business, I work with land planners, engineers, and brokers—as well as our investors.

When it comes to my Team, loyalty is a two-way street. I mentioned previously that I have told new hires, "You can tear up your resume. I don't think you'll ever be looking for another job again—so you won't be needing it." I can make this bold promise because I know enough about people before I hire them that it's clear they will be a good fit, and I can commit to meeting their needs for increased earnings and advancement. For example, I knew so much about my assistant, Denise Organ, that I would have been stunned had she not turned out to be one of my best long-term teammates ever.

Of course, there's a potential downside to this commitment, too. When the recession began in 2007—and the Arizona real estate industry suffered tremendously—I committed to my team that I would not let anyone go. Yes, everyone understood that there would be no bonuses, no pay raises, and many of the usual "El Dorado Perks" would be no more; however, everyone would continue to have a job—period. It also involved a great deal of personal cost. I was no longer able to entertain investors and promote El Dorado as I had in the past, and my personal income was substantially reduced in order to keep our employees. In retrospect, though, I've never once regretted making that promise.

Our relationship with suppliers is also a two-way street. In real estate, our suppliers are brokers, lawyers, surveyors, architects, and the like. Because our vendors know that they will benefit from new ventures, they are dedicated to giving us both the service and the quality we have come to expect. And we are committed to compensating them fairly as well as paying them on time.

Come to think of it, our relationship with investors is also a two-way arrangement. We build our company on their investments, and they expect us to provide a reasonable return on the money they invest. When we deliver, they reward us with their loyalty.

One of our first investors was Dr. Jim Little, a world-famous ophthalmologist from Oklahoma City who pioneered several major surgical procedures. He invested in our first venture, and, to this day, he's the largest investor we've ever had—and he continues to be involved in every new offering. He is now even a shareholder in our management company, El Dorado Holdings. I was happy to offer him an ownership position when he stepped up to the table during our early years and provided working capital when we needed it. That's because we both share the value of loyalty. In fact, Dr. Jim is the perfect model for an investor and a partner. No one could be any better.

When a relationship is working, there is no reason to change. In fact, true loyalty is demonstrated when a reason to change surfaces, and yet the underlying loyalty becomes the glue that helps the relationship survive. I can think of many marriages that survived seemingly unbearable hardships, yet loyalty—and love— held them together. This applies not only to my happy, long-lasting marriage to Sheila, but also to our relationships with investors and team members.

Customers fit into our company in an odd sort of way. Our actual customers—the homebuilders and commercial developers who buy the land offered by El Dorado Holdings—are the initial customers. But ultimately, our customers are the families who buy the homes, and the business customers who build or lease commercial space.

To gain the loyalty of homebuilders and commercial developers, we have to deliver on our promises—infrastructure, improvements, amenities, and the like. Loyalty on the part of families involves positive word-of-mouth. When we—and the builders—deliver on our collective promises, families will recommend our developments to their friends. Houses become homes, and homes become communities.

Loyalty, indeed, is an essential part of building any successful company.

· · · · ·

Chapter Six

THE POWER OF TRUST

A man I greatly admire (and about whom I will write later in this book), is the late S. Truett Cathy, the founder of Chick-fil-A. He is quoted as saying, "Success in any relationship or endeavor begins with trust."

I've thought long and hard about this chapter, because trust is a difficult thing to understand and explain. I think the reason is that it's so fragile.

It can take years to build trust, but the smallest thing can destroy it. Then it takes more years to rebuild it—if it ever *can* be rebuilt.

Think about these two situations: marriage and parenting teenagers.

When one of the partners in a marriage strays into an extra-marital relationship, it's almost impossible to restore trust. It takes a lot of time, a lot of counseling, and I believe, a lot of prayer. It requires an almost supernatural measure of forgiveness. I've never seen an "overnight fix" in this situation, and I've witnessed this sad story unfold in the lives of lots of friends and acquaintances.

If your teenage son or daughter breaks your trust by getting involved with drugs or alcohol, or by driving recklessly, or by committing some crime, it will invariably take a lot of time to rebuild the relationship. You will want to believe that things have changed, but there will likely always be a nagging doubt.

Of course, the obvious way to gain trust is to be trustworthy. It's as simple as that!

At El Dorado Holdings, we seek to be the trusted source of sound investment opportunities in real estate. We have investors who have signed up for every deal we've ever offered, because they know their trust is well-placed.

I had one instance where my desire to instill trust in my investors almost backfired, though.

The first time I approached Dr. Little to invest with us was when we put together our first deal. We were both very busy at the time, so we were unable to meet in person. I called him on the phone and presented the opportunity. He said, "That sounds great, Mike. I'll take a percentage of that deal."

Deb Bricker stayed up all night long and put together a very nice marketing package for Dr. Little so he could review all of the details.

He called the next day, reached Deb, and said, "I've decided not to go in on this offering, after all."

So I called him back and asked, "Jim, what's wrong? Why don't you want to invest in this project?"

He responded, "You've obviously shopped this all over the country, and you've probably come to me as a last resort."

"Why do you say that?" I asked.

"Well, you sent me this slick marketing package, so I'm guessing you've presented it far and wide."

I almost choked at that one. "No, Jim, you are the first and only person I have presented this to. Deb stayed up all night long to put together a package so you would have an idea of what you were getting into."

"Oh, okay. Well, in that case, yeah, put me in. In fact, I will double my investment." And he did.

I learned something about trust from that experience. Namely, different people have differing definitions of what it means to trust and be trusted. Dr. Little, like so many of our investors since then, likes to be in on the ground floor. Their trust is the result of being "in the know" right from the beginning.

Believe it or not, many of our most successful ventures have their beginnings in restaurants, drawn out on paper napkins. That's because paper napkins look like the ground floor, and our investors trust that!

You might guess that one of the keys to building trust is to build a relationship. Most of us have lower levels of trust for people we don't know well.

Because I enjoy rodeo, hunting, fishing, golf, and many other outdoor activities, I quite naturally attract investors who have similar interests. Of course, I use these shared interests to build relationships. From my days in wholesale distributing to today, I plan activities that include investors or even potential investors. That's how they get to know me, and it becomes the first step to earning their trust. I haven't missed a year in taking a group with me to the National Finals Rodeo, and for the past twenty-eight years, I've organized fishing trips to either Alaska or British Columbia, taking up to fifty or sixty investors with us. We've also booked numerous pheasant hunting trips to the Great State of South Dakota, and in the process have raised money for great charities including Gary Sinise Foundation, Wounded Warrior, Joe Foss Institute and Chuck Norris' Kickstart Kids.

THROUGH THE EYES OF A LOYAL INVESTOR AND FRIEND

I was introduced to Mike many years ago through a good friend of mine, Jerry Caven. Jerry had started investing with Mike and had done quite well.

At first, I was quite skeptical as Mike seemed to be just too good a salesman. It took me several years to figure out that he was for real. I very cautiously started investing in Mike's deals and found out that Jerry was right; this guy could make deals happen. After three or four years of making some nice returns and getting comfortable with Mike, I started getting some other people (including some of my employees) into Mike's investments.

In 1999, when Mike put together investors for the Circle Cross Ranch property, I made a big commitment as I thought we had our company sold (which didn't occur). I talked to Mike about reducing our portion down, but being the super salesman that he is, Mike talked me into staying in for the full amount.

When I finally saw the property several months later, I was scared to death. The property was literally in the middle of nowhere, and to top it off, we were going to have to demo a huge feedlot. Fortunately, Mike saw something there that I certainly didn't, and it ended up being the best investment we ever made! Today, we are all very appreciative of our involvement with Mike. It has been a very profitable 20+ years for all of us.

Mike and I not only became business partners, but also good friends. We rodeo, hunt, boat, and just generally have a great time together. My wife and I always enjoy spending time with Mike and Sheila.

Mike always contributes more than his fair share in whatever he does. Here's to another 20 years!

—Larry Williams

Early Partner now also Dear Friend

As I'm sure you well know, people buy from people they know, trust, and respect—and with whom they have relationships. In fact, it's known that people who give to a particular charity often do so because of the individual who leads that charity. They believe in and invest in the individual who is leading that cause.

For example, my trust in Gary Sinise (a celebrated actor who appeared in numerous productions including the movie, *FORREST GUMP*, and the hit TV series, CSI:NY, rightfully has a Star on the Hollywood Walk of Fame) has led me to support some of his wonderful causes through his creation of THE LT. DAN BAND, including The Joe Foss Foundation, the American Veterans Disabled for Life Memorial and the Navy SEAL Foundation. He also co-hosts the National Memorial Day Concert on the Mall in Washington, D.C. For his work with his Gary Sinise Foundation, including its work with smart homes for severely wounded veterans, Gary was made an honorary U.S. Navy Chief Petty Officer in 2012. In 2013, he was named an honorary Marine by the Commandant of the Marine Corps and that same year he received the third highest honor from the Department of the Army Civilian Awards, the Outstanding Civilian Service Award.

My trust in the leader—combined with my trust in the purpose, validity, and integrity of his causes—made it easy for me to become a loyal, long-term supporter of these fine organizations.

BE THE LEADER YOU SEEK

I strive to be the leader that others can trust as well. There was one trip, though, where I thought I was going to lose the trust of my investors forever. I took thirty of our investors to the Amazon River on a fishing and hunting trip. Usually the month of February is a dry season in the Amazon. But this particular year, they had the worst rain and floods that they have ever had. The Amazon was running about 14-18 feet above flood stage.

To get to the lodge, we had to travel up the river in open bass boats. By the time we got to our destination, our luggage was soaked and so were we. Humidity was hovering around 100%, so it was very difficult, if not impossible, to get anything to dry out.

Undaunted, we were ready to go fishing first thing the next morning. The manager walked up to us and told us that he had a problem—all of his fishing guides had gone on strike. So the next day we found ourselves sitting around the lodge, playing cards and telling stories. Finally they found some other guides to come in to take us fishing. However, we didn't catch a lot of fish, because the water was so high.

One day when we were out fishing, we stopped on the shore for lunch. When we returned to our boat, we didn't realize that it was taking on water. Only when we got away from the shore did we realize that we were starting to sink. To make matters worse, we didn't have any life jackets. The Amazon is so wide that we could look in both directions and couldn't see the shore. It's that huge. In fact, fifteen percent of all of the fresh water in the world comes out of the mountains and into the Amazon.

We were in a frightening situation, especially for my wife, Sheila, because she can't swim—and, of course, there was that issue of piranhas! But there she was, trying to dip water out of the boat with a Coke bottle. And the guide was in the back with a cup trying to bail water, but it was coming in faster than they could bail. We were definitely praying for help and trying to control our rising panic. Finally another boat came along and the crew threw us some life jackets and pulled us back to shore.

What a trip! It rained almost every day, our guides were on strike, we caught very few fish, we wore wet clothes for days (thanks to the humidity), and our boat nearly sank.

Then, when we got ready to leave, we were told that the only airline that services that part of Brazil, Bolivian Airlines, was also on strike. Once again, with the mantra, "Whatever it takes," we regrouped and found an alternate way home. We were forced to call in a charter service from the United States to come pick us up.

You would think it would have been the worst trip imaginable and that my thirty investors would never trust me again. In reality, it was such an indelible memory for everyone that we had t-shirts printed up that said, "Everything Strikes in the Amazon Except the Bass!"

To this day, our investors—whom I refer to as partners—still say that this was one of the greatest trips we ever had, because we all got so much better acquainted and our relationships were strengthened.

Some observers doubt that this sort of trust-building adventure can actually succeed. A good friend of mine who's in the development business ran into me and a group of my investors as we were checking into a hotel in Vancouver before a salmon fishing adventure. The first words out of his mouth were, "Mike, what on earth are you doing? Bringing your investors together is a formula for disaster. I would never get more than two of my investors together at any one time."

I replied, "Well, you know, that's just a difference in philosophy. I get the greatest joy out of bringing our investors together. We share stories, we learn from one another, and a lot of them have become great friends. I didn't plan it that way—it just worked out that way. Our investors love to associate with other very successful people."

Basically, trust is at the core of my relationship with my investors, so I have no fear of bringing them together. Everything about our partnerships is open. And because our partnerships are structured in such a way that I can be removed from my management role at any time, I have to make sure I perform at all times.

Performance, indeed, leads to trust.

A GREAT LESSON IN BEING TRUSTWORTHY

I believe this account shares a great example of a basic philosophy that helps an individual become trusted…

I had the pleasure of meeting Alphonso Jackson at the 2018 Horatio Alger's award ceremony where he was being inducted into the Society. Alphonso was the 13th US Secretary of Housing and Urban Development (HUD), nominated by President George W. Bush in 2004, serving until 2008. Alphonso started his career as an assistant professor at the University of Missouri, and since has taken on many roles in both the private and public sectors, including Executive Director of the St. Louis Housing Authority, Director of the U.S. Department of Public and Assisted Housing for Washington, D.C. and President and CEO of the Housing Authority of the City of Dallas. After leaving his position as U.S. Secretary of HUD, Alphonso returned to the private sector to become Vice-Chairman of Consumer and Community Banking with JPMorgan Chase. I was so impressed by the man and his life accomplishments.

During the Horatio Alger event, Alphonso used a quote of his that really meant a lot to me, and I hope that I handle all of my personal and business dealings in this manner. He said "Speak without being offensive, listen without being defensive, and always leave the person you are speaking to with their dignity."

• • • • •

Chapter Seven
THE POWER OF CUSTOMERS

Of all the "people relationships" I've talked about, your relationship with your customers is potentially the most volatile.

Here's why: you need your customers, but your customers may or may not need you. Chances are, they can get what they want from someone else. That's the nature of our competitive economy.

The people who invest their money with El Dorado Holdings, for example, have several other options. They can invest in stocks and bonds, in certificates of deposit, in precious metals, in oil and gas exploration, in foreign currencies, in residential/commercial real estate or rental properties, or with other companies similar to El Dorado. They can even invest in Hollywood films and theatrical productions… or a host of other ventures.

The customers who buy our land—the homebuilders and developers—need to make a profit as a result of buying it, building on it, and selling it to their customers. Those customers also have choices. They can buy existing homes or condos, they can choose to buy in other neighborhoods, or they can rent an apartment.

I've discovered over the years that customers want four basic things, no matter what they're buying:

1) A quality product;

2) A competitive price;

3) A warranty that is supported;

4) Excellent customer service.

Part Two of this book is all about Product Power. But what about the other three basic "wants?"

In terms of competitive price, there is always a delicate balance between attracting a customer through price and still making a profit on the transaction. I once heard a radio commercial for a car dealer in which the promise was, "We lose a little on every deal, but we make it up on volume." Of course, in the real world in which most businesses operate, this is absolutely absurd. If a company loses a little on every deal, they'll lose a *lot* on volume. Oddly, the promise may actually work for a car dealer, because car dealers generally make most of their money in the service department and on hold-back bonuses.

Here's where the "magic" of these four "customer wants" comes into play. If you are not offering a quality product, you will likely not stay in business unless the product you are selling has no viable competition in your market. That's why a really crummy airline that is the only one flying into a small city can survive… and charge outrageous fares.

If you offer a quality product, you likely will have to compete on price. But why, then, do more costly alternatives often succeed? Ask Apple Computer. (More on that phenomenon in the next chapter.)

On the other hand, if your product isn't highly differentiated from that of your competitors and if your price point is typical for the category, what do you do to gain a competitive edge in the minds of your potential customers?

The answer is found in the last two customer wants: a warranty that is supported and excellent customer service.

I personally know people who have the money to buy any Mercedes-Benz, BMW, Jaguar, or Cadillac that catches their eye. But instead, they bought a Hyundai because of that manufacturer's bold ten-year warranty and the support with which they back it up. Of course, if your plan is to lease or own your car for only three or four years, a ten-year warranty becomes less relevant, and excellent customer service becomes more significant.

My long-time investor and friend, Wes Adams, whom we unfortunately lost in February of 2011, often said, "In any conversation, someone is selling and someone is being sold." In any transaction, a successful outcome is based on trust and mutual respect. The party being sold has to respect the seller in order to become a customer. And the seller must earn that respect. Wes possessed "Street Smarts," something that so many of us envy. Even though Wes is now gone, fortunately he passed his business and people skills on to his sons. They have done extremely well in their business ventures.

The bottom line is that your customers are the key to your success. It takes a careful balance of key components to attract them, keep them happy, and retain them.

If companies expended as much energy in making sure that their current customers are happy as they do trying to attract new customers, they would experience much greater success. My belief is that customer and investor retention is 75% of the secret of our company's success.

• • • • •

THE SECOND KEY: PRODUCT POWER

Chapter Eight
THE POWER OF INNOVATION

As you well know, several books have been written about the creative genius of the late Steve Jobs, one of the original founders of Apple who was forced out of power in the 1980s, but made his triumphant return in the 1990's to rescue the company from the brink of demise.

Steve, of course, was not an expert on computers. He might not even have been the "nicest" guy who ever lived. I certainly would not want to emulate all of his approaches to business and to life.

But he *was* gifted with the power of innovative thinking. There were already MP3 players on the market when he guided the design of the iPod. But none was as elegant, aesthetically pleasing, or as easy to use. There were already scores of cellular phones on the market when the iPhone was released. But none so capable, so feature-rich, or again, so aesthetically pleasing. There were already tablet computers, but none as highly functioning as the iPad—thanks in part to the hundreds of thousands of Apps that had already been created for the iPhone and iPod Touch.

There are, I believe, three opportunities for innovation that every individual and every company need to explore:

1) It's never been done.
2) It's already been done, but not as well as it could be.
3) It's already been done well, but not as inexpensively or as efficiently as it could have been.

Think about the key words that have been employed in so many marketing campaigns: "NEW," "IMPROVED," and "PRICE REDUCED"—or in the latter's basic form, "ON SALE NOW."

If you're an Apple user, you know that Steve Jobs, Tim Cook, and their associates never really developed anything "completely, totally" new. And their prices certainly haven't been "lowest in the market." Most PC laptops cost about half as much as a comparable Apple MacBook.

No, if you think about it, Steve & company excelled on the second key element of innovation: "It's already been done, but not as well as it could have been."

Many people who stumble upon the Macintosh Operating System (OS) wonder why the Microsoft OS can't be as straightforward, intuitive, and crash-resistant. The answer is simple. Apple took the position that "it's already been done, but not as well as it could be." They didn't "copy" Microsoft. They innovated. In fact, it could easily be argued that Microsoft has copied Apple.

Back in an era when it wasn't really considered "sexist," there was an airline that featured female flight attendants dressed in "hot pants." It was called Southwest Airlines, and the late Herb Kelleher had ideas on how to get the business traveler hooked on his airline.

Herb differentiated Southwest Airlines from the pack. He ran an airline that was on time and very dependable. And he offered low fares that blew away the competition—and still usually do. Plus, "bags fly free"—at least I hope they still do when you read this.

But there were other things that Herb relied on to set his airline apart. He built a culture of very friendly, cheerful personnel—people who were extremely accommodating and actually acted like they appreciated your business. Except it wasn't an act.

Now, do you want to fly with somebody who behaves as though they're doing you a favor, or do you want to fly with somebody who gives you solid clues that they really appreciate the fact you're flying with them and they value your business?

It didn't take very long for Southwest Airlines to move to the top of the pack, because people love to feel like they're valued.

I have flown Southwest Airlines countless times, and I appreciate them. In these days of high technology, when you call most major airlines for a reservation, you have to punch this or that button, enter this or that code, and hope that you eventually talk to a human being. That is not the case with Southwest Airlines. Don't punch anything; just stay on the line for a few moments, and you'll talk to a real person... an actual human being who will help you.

The people at the counters are real people, too. From gate agents to baggage handlers, they are all friendly, helpful professionals. Both Sheila and I felt such a connection and appreciation for the personnel at Southwest, we organized a huge barbeque for them at our Paradise Valley home and invited all of the Phoenix crew. The event was very well attended and included everyone from gate personnel, baggage handlers and even pilots. Many of my El Dorado staff were also in attendance to show their appreciation to these fine people.

It's been amazing to me that, as much as they've grown, they've still been able to maintain that personal touch. Of course, you're going to get a bad apple every now and then. One of my favorite Zig Ziglar quotes from his book, *SEE YOU AT THE TOP*, is, "Some people look like someone has licked all the red off their candy."

Southwest Airlines was never concerned about doing something that had never been done before. Other airlines had been around for years before Southwest entered the arena. But they wisely focused on the other two keys to innovation: doing it better and doing it cheaper and more efficiently. As long as they pay attention to those two things, they will be a standout in the industry.

Over the years, I've had to determine which of the principles of innovation applied to my business, El Dorado Holdings, Inc.

I concluded that, for land developers, all three aspects of innovation come into play:

- It's never been done.
- It's already been done, but not as well as it could be.
- It's already been done well, but not as inexpensively or as efficiently as it could be.

El Dorado Holdings had its beginnings in 1987 with one escrow property south of Phoenix—which happened to be one of the ranches that the famous actor John Wayne owned for over 42 years—the El Dorado Ranch. I was averse to bank debt, so, instead, I raised the money through investors to close on the property. My new company was off and running. Or so I thought.

Within a year of my great purchase, the real estate market in Phoenix started to flounder, and I was deeply concerned that I wouldn't survive the downturn and I would lose all my investors' money. El Dorado was founded on a "wing and a prayer," so we did not have much in the way of reserves. Without sales, our rapidly diminishing coffers would soon be empty. Our telephones quit ringing, and when we would call other companies with which we did business—consultants, brokers, engineers, surveyors, and so on—many times we would be greeted by that automated reply stating, "This number is no longer in service." Companies, especially those involved with real estate, were going under in record numbers.

But, thankfully, another thing happened in the late 80s that helped me not only weather the downturn but create great new opportunities for my company.

I discovered the Resolution Trust Corporation (RTC), the government entity formed to manage the failed bank and savings and loan institutions. They "managed" them by selling off their assets at incredible discounts to value. Amazingly, I was able to gather a group of investors who believed with me that Phoenix would weather this storm. They stuck with me, and as a result, I began buying properties at astoundingly low prices through the RTC. One of those investors was Dalton Knauss. I'm honored to say he is still a loyal El Dorado investor. Dalton started his career in his garage working in electronics, building his small undertaking into a very successful business and ultimately selling this company to Square D. I remember clearly Dalton telling me "Mike, you got this buying down, but when are you going to learn to sell?" In response, I told Dalton there is a time to buy and a time to sell.

Thank goodness, a time to sell came along.

Many of these investments began making a profit almost immediately, and that helped take the pressure off the need to make money on El Dorado Ranch right way.

For us, innovation involved finding ways to protect the investments we had already made by making significant new investments during a time of economic decline.

There are all sorts of ways to innovate.

- Innovative ideas solve a need.
- Innovative customer service builds loyalty and repeat business.
- Innovation adds value… and this turned out to be very important when it came to developing our properties.

Innovation is important in the advancement of anyone's vision and effectiveness, whether it's the kind of innovation that helps pastors and rabbis communicate with their congregations, or teachers with their students, or even parents with their children.

I believe most people who are looking to do a better job and create better products and services will be innovators. Then, after innovation's done, you'll need to find the leaders to guide and motivate the rest of the team…and the team members themselves to work on those innovative ideas and turn them into reality.

When talking about innovation, my association with the Arizona Diamondbacks organization comes to my mind. Approximately ten years ago, the El Dorado partners, who were, at the time, Dr. Jim Little, Monty Ortman, and me, were approached by the Diamondbacks about investing in the ball club. Dr. Little was somewhat hesitant about joining in since he lives in Oklahoma and wouldn't be able to attend many games. But being the team player that he always is, he said, "Mike, if you and Monty want to do this, count me in."

We took the Diamondbacks up on their offer. However, not one of us did so thinking that this would be a great investment in terms of any monetary return on our dollars invested. We did it because we all believed that the Diamondbacks team was important for the state of Arizona and the quality of life for its residents. When promoting the Phoenix area, we would proudly be able to say that we have four major league sport teams—representing the NFL, NHL, NBA, and Major League Baseball (MLB). Not many cities can boast that fact.

The Diamondbacks, led by President Derrick Hall, have employed so many innovative ideas. As the result of their innovation, they have built fan loyalty, a cross-section of sponsorship, and fan involvement. It would literally take a whole book to tell their story. In fact, I will recommend to Derrick that he do just that.

Of course, with regard to the Diamondbacks' success, it helps if you're winning. Derrick, Ken Kendrick, and the whole front office have put together a great plan, and Torey Lovullo and the team do the rest on the field.

One of my great joys of life was being there for all seven games of the 2001 World Series—as the Diamondbacks, with two great pitchers, Randy Johnson and Curt Schilling, won the first two games in Phoenix, then travelled to New York City only to lose all three games, most in extra innings. They returned home down 3 to 2. They won the 6th game easily but game 7 came down to the last inning. At the bottom of the 9th, Louis Gonzales ("Gonzo") hit a blooper to win.

If you are not the "Steve Jobs" within your organization (or someone who "swings a great bat"), it's important that you find that person. Not in every sense, but at least in the sense that every company needs an innovator, whether it's an internal person or group, or an outside consultant or consulting firm. Innovation is the first step in creating a product or service that stands out from the crowd.

· · · · ·

Chapter Nine

THE POWER OF DESIGN

Most people can tell the difference between good design and poor design. We can tell the difference between beautiful and ugly. Between useful and useless. Between well-crafted and poorly made.

Here's an example: for many years, the standard in automobile design and manufacturing was set by foreign competitors—Mercedes-Benz, Toyota, Honda, BMW, Volvo, and the like. They won their reputation on design, quality, and endurance… not to mention resale value.

Thankfully, American automobile manufacturers have recaptured the greatness upon which they were originally founded. I am proud to drive my recent-model American-designed-and-built cars and trucks. The only way you're going to take my pickup truck away from me is to pry my cold, dead fingers off the steering wheel! I can't tell you what a kick I get when I pull my big white Ford F-250 Diesel up to some fancy restaurant or event with all of the Bentleys, BMWs, and Mercedes, and all of the valets fight over who gets to park my truck!

For me, and for most car, truck, and SUV buyers, it comes down to the basic elements of design:

• Beautiful;

- Useful;
- Efficient/economical;
- Well-made.

At the core of all this is a simple idea: good design creates value.

I define value as "a fair price paid for a quality product, supported by great customer service." Standards are set, and those standards are met.

There are three kinds of customers engaged in the free enterprise system:

1) Those who get less than they pay for,
2) Those who get exactly what they pay for, and
3) Those who get more than they pay for.

The true power of design—and therefore, the power of "value"—is that we, as individuals and companies, can join the group that expects and receives more than we pay for. We can also give our customers more than they expect or pay for.

As I mentioned in the last section, our first investment in the Phoenix area was a large parcel of land that was owned by the legendary John Wayne. The name of his ranch, El Dorado Ranch, is what led to the name of our company. Located just south of the small, unincorporated town of Maricopa. it's no exaggeration to say that at that time Maricopa was a mere dot on the map surrounded by cotton fields and cacti.

Shortly after that purchase, we also bought his adjacent property, Red River Ranch. Next, we purchased several farms north of Maricopa. We decided to focus on developing those northern properties first, because they were closer to Interstate 10 and closer to Phoenix with its growing southern suburbs. This development became known as Rancho El Dorado.

Now, this will sound contradictory, but although this land was useful as farmland, it was basically useless for development. It was in the middle of nowhere, surrounded by parched desert, and had poor access and no services or utilities.

However, we knew we could transform it into something beautiful, useful, and perfectly made for a specific purpose. We knew that, through the power of design, we could transform that dry, parched land into an attractive, desirable residential community.

We also knew we needed a great team leader to head up the project. We turned to Mike Reinbold. Mike had a tremendous amount of experience in development. He could easily see the vision we had, because he had worked on similar projects in Southern California. He was the right person at the right time to join our team and make our dream and vision a reality and a huge success. In addition to having our vision, Mike has the ability to accept any challenge thrown at him and deal with it. I've never heard him say, "This can't be done." It's always, "This is how we are going to get this done."

We announced our plan. And people laughed. The media mocked us. The few residents of Maricopa thought we were out of our collective heads. The newspaper reported that we planned to build a residential area, miles from the city proper, and miles from a real freeway. No one believed it would work. But I did, my team did, and our investors did.

The first challenge we faced was the road… or, rather, the lack of a road. The tiny town of Maricopa was served by a narrow, two-lane county road that was very poorly maintained. It was accessed by an exit from Interstate 10 between Phoenix and Tucson and served as a shortcut to Interstate 8 and San Diego. Miles after taking this exit, drivers would pass through Maricopa, a town that boasted little more than a gas station, a restaurant, a couple churches, a couple bars, and a small public school. Fewer than 500 residents called it home. In fact, there was no local government, no mayor, no city council, no police department, and only a small volunteer fire department. There wasn't even a hospital or a shopping center.

The first thing we decided was that we needed to create a "real" road—four lanes wide—between the freeway exit and the town. This was a daunting task for several reasons, not the least of which was the fact that we'd have to deal with and gain cooperation from eight separate groups: private, city, county, state, federal government entities, and numerous Native American tribal organizations.

To help gather support from the private sector, two prominent successful local farmers, Bill Scott and John Smith, came to my aid and were instrumental in helping me form the Maricopa Road Association. We also gained the support of Donovan Kramer, Sr., publisher of the *Casa Grande Dispatch*, the only local newspaper to service this area. The Maricopa Road Association was made up of local residents who were concerned about the road's safety. Without the hard work of these dedicated people, my role in this would have been a great deal more difficult.

The road project was fortunate to have great community leadership behind it, including Supervisor Dean Weatherly of Pinal County, Supervisor Tom Freestone of Maricopa County, Tom White, Cecil Antone, and Mary Thomas of the Gila River Indian Community, Delia Carlyle and Leona Kakar of the Ak-Chin Indian Community, Charlie Miller of the Arizona Department of Transportation (ADOT), U.S. Senator Dennis Deconcini, and scores of private citizens. We also had the support of key state legislators, including Senator Alan Stephens, and Representatives Jim Hartegen and Henry Evans. Any one of these individuals or groups could have single-handedly killed the John Wayne Parkway—State Route 347.

After years of hard work and endless meetings, we reached an agreement, broke ground in 1989, and started building the road to Maricopa in 1990.

The media loved this! They sarcastically referred to it as "The Road to Nowhere."

I'm reminded of something my friend, and a man I much admire, T. Boone Pickens, was told by his dad when young Boone was floundering in college: "A fool with a plan can achieve more than a genius with no plan." The media thought we at El Dorado Holdings were fools, but we had a plan, and we accomplished what we set out to do. The road was completed in 1996, and that's when things began to change!

The next step was to design the kind of community we believed families would actually want to call home. We knew that we had a competitive edge in pricing, because home sites in this remote area could be sold for much less than lots that were within, or closer to, the Greater Phoenix Area.

Our design plan included parks, hiking trails, a golf course, recreational facilities, and land set aside for commercial ventures, schools, and public buildings. This plan became Rancho El Dorado, the first master-planned community in Pinal County.

Fortunately, we had good people behind the plan. Alma Farrell, who owned a restaurant in the tiny town of Maricopa and also served as the superintendent of the small K-12 school, got solidly behind us, as did her son, Edward. They began the process of incorporating the town as a city, and Edward served as its first mayor. He continued to serve on the city council for many years after that. Tony Smith and Christian Price were two other Maricopa mayors who stood with us and supported our plans.

All of the elements of good design came together in the ranches of Maricopa. It was beautiful, it was useful, it was efficient and economical, and it was well made. The families who purchased new homes in Maricopa knew that they were benefitting from the power of design.

Early in the process, our critics had a field day. But as the "Road to Nowhere" began to lead to somewhere, the ridicule slowly died away. A fool with a solid Master Plan—and good design—had won them over. Maricopa, Arizona, a town of only 400 just twenty-something years ago has grown into a community of nearly 50,000 residents, and it even survived the "Sub-Prime Crash" a few years ago. Banner Health Hospital and Central Arizona College, as well as three shopping areas, numerous restaurants, grocery stores—including a Walmart—are open and thriving.

Our next task in this unfolding story of design and transformation was to "add value…."

· · · · ·

Chapter Ten
THE POWER OF ADDING VALUE

The concept of adding value is very simple: take something good and make it better: make it worth more, whether it's real worth or perceived worth.

Sometimes the simplest ideas can transform good to better.

With the "Road to Nowhere" completed, we were able to begin to implement our plans and designs. That's when Mike Reinbold's talent really added value. The Master Plan called for all sorts of value-added features… main corridors lined with majestic palm trees, attractive street lighting, underground utility service, curbs and gutters, golf courses, and other features.

Our underlying objective was to create an attractive, desirable, affordable suburban community. We knew we could not adopt the standards that are evident in the most luxurious parts of Scottsdale, or Palm Desert or Beverly Hills. Yet, we wanted to make sure that our new development in Maricopa was comparable to what you might see in any very upscale development in the Southeast Valley of Phoenix.

We had toured other recent developments in outlying areas and we made a list of things that they had, in our opinion, done poorly.

One particular community had open carports attached to the houses. We demanded that our builders include a minimum of a two-car garage in all their plans. No carports. No roof-top air conditioning units, either.

That same community allowed composite shingle roofs: we insisted that all roofs be tile. They permitted rooftop-mounted heating and cooling units… a much cheaper way to install the unit. We insisted that all units be at ground level and concealed by fencing.

The other community we checked out had a golf course but wasn't really a championship-style golf course. It didn't have the lighting or the landscaping. Many of the streets weren't paved, there were no sidewalks, and the setbacks from the street were not as great as what we planned. The building codes were not strict.

We decided to hold our builders to a higher standard. Some of them said, "Guys, we want to build one-thousand-square-foot homes or less." We said, "No home can be smaller than 1400 square feet." These were the same standards you would see in the Cities of Chandler or Gilbert, two suburbs of Phoenix. They were higher standards than those required by the county. Today, the city of Maricopa has very stringent standards—as stringent as any community in the Phoenix area. It was these standards that added value for homeowners.

Another key aspect of adding value is to create partnerships with organizations to benefit our customers. We worked with others to provide key services: electricity, cable TV, fiber optics phone service, and transportation. In fact, without these essential partnerships, we wouldn't have any customers—we wouldn't have a vibrant community today.

The first issue we encountered was that there was no infrastructure to provide electrical power—and no one wanted to provide it. The big players thought it would not be economically feasible. In their defense, they really had no idea that we intended to transform this sleepy community of 500 into a thriving mini-metropolis of 200,000 or more. By 2019, Maricopa's estimated population was 50,024 according to the most recent United States census information… well on its way to our vision!

Since Arizona Public Service (APS) nor any other of the big utility companies showed any interest in servicing this area, we developed a new electrical power utility in cooperation with Southern California Edison and Electric District 3 (ED3), a rural electric cooperative.

For years, local farmers had secured more than adequate power from ED3. However, as farming scaled back, more than enough power could be made available for this new community.

So, in cooperation with Edison, we went into the electrical power business. Edison had the capital, they had the knowledge, and ED3 had cheap hydroelectric power that they had contracted years ago to meet the farmers' needs—power from the Hoover Dam, for example. Because of dwindling need, they were able to convert that power to residential customers, commercial customers, and industrial customers in our new development.

I'm sure that, today, the big power companies regret their decision not to service us. They were not willing to beef up their capacity because they believed that our project would quickly go bankrupt and the risk was too great.

We faced a similar situation with water and wastewater. No existing utility was willing to serve us, so we had to start our own water and wastewater company.

The same thing was true with cable television service. The local provider, Cox, chose not to provide service, so we partnered with a company called Orbital to bring cable TV service to our community.

Once all of these utilities were secured, we started digging, we buried all the pipes and cables, and brought them to the lot lines so that builders could connect to the new homes they were selling.

Without all this value-added effort, the 1,100 home lots that were in escrow could never have been sold and built upon.

As time went on, I was approached by another utility company that offered to buy out our utility services company. Since I never wanted to be in the utility business in the first place, I sold it to them for a very nice profit.

I didn't want to be in the railroad business, either, but it became apparent that value would be added to our developments if we could offer Amtrak rail service. Service to central Phoenix was going to be shut down, so the closest possible train station was an old abandoned station in Casa Grande, which was twice as far from Phoenix as Maricopa.

As a result of our perceived need for passenger service, we formed a public/private partnership with Pinal County back in 2000. Before we could offer that "value-added feature," we had to find the money. We located a federal grant to help fund it, I had to put up some of the money, and Pinal County also put some money into the project. Most of it, however, came from a federal grant.

The project was guided by Deb Bricker in our office, who worked with Brad Gair, the Pinal County Public Works Director, and the Pinal County Board of Supervisors, who had helped us get the funds put in place.

We then sought out and once again found the support we needed to locate the Phoenix terminal for Amtrak in Maricopa.

To add additional "transportation value," we found an old California Zephyr sleeping car in Indianapolis. We purchased it, transported it to Chicago where we had it beautifully refurbished and then moved by rail to Maricopa. That refurbished Zephyr became the ticket office and waiting area for Amtrak passengers. When Amtrak later built their new facility, the California Zephyr was retired and now houses the Maricopa Historical Society Museum. However, to this day, if you want to take the train to or from Phoenix, you will board Amtrak in the City of Maricopa.

Very clearly, all of these carefully laid plans and worthy designs added value, because they made good things better. Adding Value takes Creativity!

• • • • •

Chapter Eleven

THE POWER OF CREATIVE MARKETING

You have probably figured out by now that Zig Ziglar was a long-time close friend of mine, as well as a confidante and a trusted mentor. Yes, I will always be proud to have known him and his wife Jean, whom he affectionately called "The Redhead." I worked closely with him for many years. In fact, it was Zig who introduced me to the Horatio Alger Award, of which he was a past winner. (This award is bestowed on individuals who—through determination and hard work—have risen from abject poverty to become successes in their fields of endeavor.)

Zig always loved my stories about marketing, so he suggested that I write a book about "creative marketing." That was my original intent when I started working on this book, but it quickly occurred to me that there are many additional principles that I have always tried to apply in my life. That's how this book became "*THE MASTER PLAN.*"

But in Zig's honor, I am going to give special attention to the principles of creative marketing, because creative marketing, in my case, is an essential element of success.

The first thing I learned about creative marketing is: *If you find a way to give your customers something of real value, they will want more of it.*

I trace my marketing philosophy back to my early working days. After graduating from college, I accepted a position with America's Stores Packing Company. I was there for only two years, but they offered me a great deal of experience. Working in a meat packing plant was definitely not my passion, and I really didn't enjoy it. I believe it's important to "love your work," even though we all know that "work will never love you back."

TEN BY TEN

It was while working for America's Stores that I picked up an evening and weekend sales position with Kirby vacuum cleaners—yes, doing those in-home demonstrations. In my opinion Kirby, was, and is, a great company, because they really do make a great product.

My Kirby office would obtain leads and turn those leads over to a team of salespeople. Most of the sales staff was older than I was, and they had been selling Kirby products for years. They wanted the "easy" sales. They would scour the leads and choose those customers who wanted "Free Offer A."

At the time, Kirby had two offers to entice potential customers to invite us into their homes. "Free Offer A" was a set of steak knives. "Show me your vacuum cleaner, give me my knives, please, and leave." "Free Offer B" involved the salesperson shampooing a 10-foot by 10-foot area of the prospect's carpeting to demonstrate the power and efficiency of the Kirby system.

By the time I arrived at the office after my "day job," I was pleased to discover that the experienced salespeople had passed over the prospects who had chosen "Free Offer B"—the ten by ten carpet shampoo. Of course, the other salespeople preferred to deliver knives rather than having to work harder to shampoo a carpet.

Armed with the best equipment money could buy, I would knock on doors and announce, "I'm here to clean a ten-foot by ten-foot area of your carpet. Where would you like me to do this?"

Invariably, the prospect would lead me into a room that was 12 by 16 or 16 by 20. (There are very few rooms that are actually 10 by 10.)

I would mark out an area that was 10 by 10, vacuum it thoroughly, and then shampoo it. They would watch intently.

The results were amazing! Carpet that was having a near-death experience would come back to life! "What do you think?" I'd ask.

"Amazing," they'd reply. "But, um, now only that little 10 by 10 area is clean. What about the rest of it?"

Bingo! Another sale! I quickly became Kirby's number one salesperson in the area, because I took on the prospects that involved actual work, and because I learned that if I gave customers something good, they would want more of it!

(Now I admit there were more than a few times when an elderly prospect simply couldn't afford a shiny new Kirby with all the attachments, so I would either stay behind and finish shampooing the carpet or, if I had another appointment, I would volunteer to come back. There were two reputations on the line—Kirby's and mine. "Stranding" people is not the way to build a good reputation for anyone.)

The second thing I learned about creative marketing is: *If you have a quality product, creative marketing can help you introduce it to new markets.*

SPOT ON!

One of my good friends is a wonderful man by the name of Barry Meguiar. Many of you probably know Barry as the gregarious host of Speed Channel's (now "Discovery Velocity") television show, "Car Crazy," which was on the air from 2009 to 2015, and during which Barry interviewed automotive enthusiasts from all over the world. Barry's grandfather started a company called "Meguiar's Wax" back in the early 1900s. This was a high-quality wax that was used by furniture manufacturers to protect their lacquered furniture. It was only sold to furniture makers: that was its only market.

A few years later, the automobile industry was born, and the cars were painted with lacquer. Grandpa Meguiar started selling his product to Ford Motor Company and other early car builders.

That was the beginning of creative marketing for Meguiar's… but there's more.

After opening up the automobile market for a furniture wax, Meguiars began selling their wax to automotive body shops. But still, all sales were within the industry, to professionals.

Then Barry got involved in the family business in sales. Barry is an admitted "car guy." He's one of those people who love the sculptured look, the smell, the sound, and the power of a beautiful automobile. He must certainly be one of the guys about whom The Beach Boys wrote their hit songs such as "409" and "Little Deuce Coupe."

Several years ago, Barry got hooked on exotic car auctions, such as the famous Barrett-Jackson shows in Scottsdale, AZ; Palm Beach, FL; Orange, CA; and Las Vegas, NV.

One fine day, Barry went to a show and took several cans of Meguiar's wax with him. He asked the owner of a very expensive car that was being prepped for auction if he could demonstrate his wax. The owner said yes, so Barry waxed an area about a foot in diameter, then asked, "What do you think?"

The owner said, "Wow! But now the rest of the car looks dull. What am I supposed to do about that?"

Barry replied, "Tell you what. I'll give you the remaining wax so you can finish polishing your car. But I'd like you to put a sign in your window that reads, 'Shine by Meguiar's Wax.'"

Barry then moved on to the next car in the show area. Then the next. And the next. By the time he had finished his rounds, nearly every car on the lot had Meguiar's wax on the body, and a Meguiar's sign in the window.

A huge new market was born. Today, Barry's products are arguably the most respected in the industry. I call his great, innovative technique "Spot On Marketing."

I'm sure you've noticed that both of these stories have a few things in common:

1) A convincing demonstration of a quality product;
2) The customer's desire for more; and,
3) A readily available solution, offered without delay.

But you might be saying, "There's a fourth thing. You both blackmailed your prospects. You shampooed a 10 by 10 area. Barry waxed a tiny spot on a big car."

I believe the difference between creative marketing and blackmail is very clear. Creative marketing arrives at one's door dressed as "ethics." As "integrity."

A creative marketer never strands the customer in an uncomfortable position.

A creative marketer always identifies a customer's true needs and wants.

A creative marketer always leaves a satisfied customer behind.

Yes, I shampooed a 10 by 10 area. But even if the customer could not afford to buy a Kirby—or didn't want to buy one—I finished the job. Yes, Barry waxed a small section of a show car, after getting the owner's permission to do so. But he also gave the owner free wax. Every aspect of each arrangement was based on a fair trade, I believe.

In both cases, customers' needs and wants were identified. In my case, a clean home was a significant desire of my prospects. In Barry's case, a shiny, sparkling car was in a better position to draw top dollar in an auction.

In both cases, customers were satisfied… either by service or a quality product… or both.

Here, then, is the third principle and the third story in this chapter.

The third principle: *Creative marketing means identifying what the customer really wants or needs—then delivering on it in unforgettable ways.*

RAT BAIT

I've told you about my years with Tufts & Son of Oklahoma. In many respects, John Tufts, Sr. was also a father to me, as was Virgil Haley, who was a powerful influence in my life after my father died. John gave me the opportunity to be the sales force for our new company in the state of Oklahoma. Up to that point in my life, this seemed like my dream career: I owned 50% of my future!

John was one of the wisest men I have ever met. He told me, "The people who can do it can't tell you how to do it. Those who can tell you how to do it can't do it." I think he may have misjudged himself, though. He could both do it, and tell me how to do it.

Our company sold animal health-related products and vet medicine to farm stores, feed stores, veterinarians, and co-ops. We would buy from manufacturers and sell to the retail outlets. They, in turn, would sell the products to farmers and ranchers.

Of course, one of the ongoing problems farmers and ranchers face is that of controlling pests. And among the major pests they have to deal with are rats and mice—ugly, dirty, destructive, contaminated rodents. To do so, they relied on rat bait. You've likely heard of d-CON®, I'm sure. It's the standard rat bait containing Warfarin. Along came a brand-new rat bait with the exact chemical found in d-CON. It was manufactured by Hess & Clark, who owned the patent to Warfarin.

Now, of course, we had a lot of our competitors in the field, and many of them also sold Hess & Clark products.

Hess & Clark made an introductory offer to us that we, in turn, could offer to our customers: "If you buy two cases, you get one case free." The basic idea was that this would encourage salespeople to offer a discount to customers—which they did. So we knew our competitors would pounce on our existing customers with this offer to try to win their other business away from us as well.

I spent some time thinking about ways to set ourselves apart from our competition. The manufacturer offered two different package sizes. They had a 3-pound bulk pack containing "throw packs" that sold to the dealers wholesale for $12 a case, and they had a 1-pound size packaged 20 to a case that sold for $20 a case. My question to the manufacturer was, "If I buy two cases of the 3-pound size which had a dealer cost of $12, can I take my free goods in the more expensive 1-pound, $20 dealer cost case size?"

They informed me, "No, you'll have to take your free goods in the same size that you buy the first two."

I asked, "What if I buy 500 cases?"

The salesman checked with his sales manager in Ohio and it was decided if I bought 500 cases they would let me take my free goods however I wanted them. For every two cases of the throw packs, which sold to the dealer for $12 each, I took my free goods in the 1-pound size that I sold to the dealer for $20 each.

Instead of simply giving them free product with each purchase as my competition was offering, I decided to offer them something completely different… something really exciting! So I went to Winchester Arms, the gun manufacturer and told them I wanted to buy Winchester Model 190 .22 caliber semi-automatic rifles and give them away as a premium gift. These rifles sold for between $88 and $92 retail, depending on whether there was a special on them. Winchester agreed to let us buy them in lots of 100. They would ship them to me through their distributor at the cost of $30. Now, I had a way to drive the rat bait business!

I'd walk into the dealer carrying packages of Hess & Clark's new rat bait, Warfarat, in one hand, and a brand new Winchester .22 rifle under the other arm, and I'd present my card—"Tufts & Son of Oklahoma." If you know anything about rural America, you know that rifles are a really big deal. It doesn't matter if you already own a semi-automatic .22 rifle, you always would like to have one more.

It was something to see! The dealers would leave paying customers standing at the cash register so they could come over to see what I had. The same dealers who hadn't given me the time of day on the last call, came over and asked, "What's the deal with the rifle?"

I'd answer, "I've got a promotion you're going to remember. Whether you buy it or not, I guarantee you'll remember it."

"OK, let's see it!" they'd say.

I'd explain, "Hess & Clark has a brand-new rat bait that contains Warfarin, just like the product you have on your shelf. I want you to buy four cases of these new little throw packs of rat bait. Your cost is $12 a case, so that's $48 (4 X $12) worth of rat bait. I also want you to buy two cases of the 1-pound size, just like the d-CON product you have on your shelf today. Those two cases will cost you $40, (2 X $20) so your total cost is $88. Now, when you buy this, you're going to receive a Winchester 190 .22 semi-automatic rifle with a 4-power scope absolutely free, along with your 6 cases of the best rat bait made."

They'd look at me, they'd look at my card, they'd look at me again, and they'd say, "Son, I'm going to try you just this one time. This deal better be just like you said it was, or I'm going to get a gun and I'm going to find you."

I heard that time and time again. Yet, they bought every time, because I was giving them a $90 rifle with an $88 purchase of rat bait. They were getting six cases of rat bait for $88—with a rifle that was worth $90 thrown in.

Remember, this rifle cost me $30. I bought it with the $40 they paid me for my free goods, leaving a $10 extra profit per deal for me. On top of that, I was also making my regular profit on my 4 cases of throw packs. It was a very profitable transaction for me. I never made a presentation—ever—that I didn't sell a rat bait deal.

Sometimes, the customers would ask, "Are you sure this rat bait's any good?" Then they would think for a minute and say, "Aw, well, never mind. If it isn't, I've got a rifle and I'll shoot them."

During this time, two of the best peddlers this world has ever known joined me. Ed Jessup and Sam Holman became part of a very successful team that eventually grew to six people strong in Oklahoma alone.

We were shipping out rifles left and right, and we made sure the customers got their rifles even before the rat bait came in.

Soon we were on our third rail carload of rat bait. We delivered more than 500 rifles, and we were attracting new customers every day.

One day I was getting ready to go on a sales call when I saw a black car pull up in front of our office. Two guys in suits stepped out of the car, and Sheila came into my office and said, "There are two men out there with badges, and they'd like to talk to you."

They came into my office and showed me their credentials. They were with the Department of Alcohol, Tobacco, and Firearms, and they were "visiting" from Dallas, Texas. They wanted to know what my intent was with the 500 rifles I had purchased.

I asked them to sit down, I pulled out my detail book, I showed them the rat bait deal, and I went through all the details of the transaction. They looked at each other. Then one of them turned to me and asked, "Could we buy a rat bait deal?"

I replied, "No, you can't buy a rat bait deal—we sell strictly to wholesale customers with sales tax numbers. But I can give you a copy of our sales flier for your records."

They said, "That would really help. The guys back in the office will never believe this story."

So, I gave them a copy of the deal and I said, "I'll do one more thing for you." Throughout the promotion, I had asked Sheila to keep a list of names and driver's license numbers of everyone who received a gun, just in case this question would ever come up. I asked them, "Would you like that list?" They said, "Yes," so I gave it to them.

They got up, put their suit coats back on, went out the door laughing all the way, got in their car, and drove back to Dallas.

I need to say a special "thank you" to Rod Reinke, the Hess & Clark rep, for helping make me the "Number One Rat Bait Salesman in America," as proclaimed by Zig Ziglar.

"BOOTING UP"

After that promotion wound down, I decided to try something new and connected with Tony Lama, Jr., the famous boot maker, to talk about offering his cowboy boots. Boots are like .22 rifles, in that you can always use at least one more pair. If you wear boots, you know that you can't have too many.

Their sales rep at that time was Lynn Laske. Even after I told him how successful I'd been with the rifles, Tony Lama didn't really want to cut me a deal with boots because he didn't want me competing with Sheplers, one of their major retail customers. I told them, "I will never *sell* your boots to anyone. If you ever have one complaint from Sheplers, I will understand, and the deal's off."

After much persuading by Lynn, Tony agreed to set me up and I was able to buy cowhide boots that were worth $100 for $30. I was also buying lizard and ostrich boots at well below their retail price.

For this promotion, I put together a deal with Pfizer that was very similar to the rat bait offer. Every fall, Pfizer came out with a special on Terramycin 500-milliliter bottles. This is liquid injectable oxytetracycline and it is the standard in the veterinary industry.

Pfizer was offering a 10% fall promotion discount, so my competition was out selling a five-case deal that cost the dealer

$500, or $100 per case. They were offering the dealer a 10% or $50 discount.

Instead of giving the dealers a $50 discount, I showed them a Tony Lama catalog. I was selling them the same product as my competition, but instead of giving them a $50 discount on a $500 order I was giving them a $100 pair of boots for which I was paying $30. Of course, the dealers would look at it and quickly decide they wanted a $100 pair of boots instead of a $50 discount.

They also had to decide if they wanted 5 cases, 10 cases, or 20 cases, because if their business justified it, they could get a pair of lizard boots with a 10-case order, or they could get a pair of ostrich boots with a 20-case order.

I was giving away boots left and right, of course. We were using creative marketing to differentiate ourselves from our competitors and make a higher profit at the same time.

CB RADIOS AND COWBOY HATS

Following that promotion, I made a very similar offer with a product from Cobra—CB radios. In that time before cell phones, CB radios were very popular. Every person you met—husband, wife, and kid—had a CB radio. Cobra was the top of the line.

From there I went to Stetson hats…and on and on.

THE "PERFECT" PROMOTION

During this whole process, I also discovered that the National Finals Rodeo was a very hot ticket item in Oklahoma.

I had been asked to help promote this event, so I challenged myself to come up with something "out of the box" again. This was timed in conjunction with an open house for a new warehouse I'd just built in Oklahoma City for our ever-expanding company. I bought 1100 tickets and decided to put on a trade show. The idea was to invite all the manufacturers to set up booths to display their products.

The trade show was such a huge success that I decided to make it an annual event and call it the Tufts & Son Annual Trade Show. I would sell display space to about 300 manufacturers who would come and show their products.

I invited my customers to come in and meet with the manufacturers and receive some great discounts. Not only would they get those discounts, but they also had great entertainment because, on Friday night before the rodeo started, I would bring in Grand Ole Opry stars direct from Nashville and I'd throw a big barbeque. Then I would take our top 1100 customers to the rodeo.

This trade show was so successful it became the standard in the nation. We were writing millions of dollars of business in a two-day period—Friday and Saturday—in the first part of December.

I have demonstrated again and again—as have many other successful business people—that creative marketing can give every business an unbeatable edge!

Hal Morris is a perfect example.

THE AIRPLANE TO NOWHERE

Many of my friends today are men I met as a youth. I would earn my own way each summer to summer camp in New Mexico. It was at camp that I met young Hal Morris, who would later become a close friend during my freshman year at college.

Hal didn't come from a family with money, so he knew that he'd have to be very creative to pay for his education. And he was creative! He would drive down to Mexico and purchase paintings that were done on black velvet. (I'm sure you've seen them… Elvis Presley is one popular subject.) He convinced a storeowner near the college he attended in California to take the paintings on consignment, and then he'd split the profits with the store.

This worked out well for Hal, despite all the laughter and ridicule the other students heaped on him.

But conventional college studies did not appeal to him. Instead, Hal discovered that he had a natural aptitude for real estate and the stock market. He studied hard, applied for, and got a job with Paine Webber Jackson & Curtis (now UBS AG). One of the first things he did was ask for the names of the ten most successful brokers. Then he called them and secured interviews with four of the top ten.

One of them, a young broker from California, shared a secret with him. "Fake it until you make it." He told Hal that when the markets closed at 1:00 p.m., he would hustle over to Santa Anita Race Track, Hollywood Park, or Del Mar, still in his three-piece suit. There, he would sit in his box seat and place tiny bets in the Jockey Club. Other race fans were wealthier, so they would place larger bets—but they never knew the small amount the young broker was betting.

They began to notice him, and, one by one, asked him what he did for a living. "I'm a stockbroker," he replied. "Well, you must be really successful if you can be at the race track every day," they observed.

Slowly, but most surely, the people who frequented the track became his customers, and he was enormously successful.

Hal took his cue from this lesson and decided that he would offer free investment seminars in smaller towns that were not served by investment counselors or brokerage houses. One such town within easy traveling distance was Lake Havasu, Arizona, on the California/Arizona border. Hal knew from his research that numerous wealthy people had retired there.

He would take out an ad in the local paper: "Hal Morris will be flying into Lake Havasu this Wednesday for a FREE Investment Seminar at the Holiday Inn."

The fact that someone would actually charter a plane and fly into their little town to offer a free seminar intrigued the locals, so they would check it out. Hal would pick four stocks during each visit, and ask the attendees to track them and report back the next time he flew in. Hal had done his research, often even talking to the presidents of the companies whose stocks he had picked, and, sure enough, those stocks would go up. This impressed the residents of Lake Havasu, and many of them became his loyal customers. Hal built a huge and successful career by applying the three principles of creative marketing:

- Hal found a way to give his customers *something of real value*, and they wanted more of it;
- He discovered that because he had a *quality product*, creative marketing could help him introduce it to new markets; and,
- He learned that creative marketing meant *identifying what the customer really wants or needs*—then *delivering on it in unforgettable ways.*

As the result of his success, Hal Morris has appeared on major cable network financial programs—including MSNBC, CNN, and others—and the Wall Street Journal referred to him as the "Wunderkind of Wall Street."

I have long been inspired by people like Barry Meguiar and Hal Morris, because they demonstrate that success is within reach of all of us, no matter our upbringing, education, or passions.

There are always ways to separate yourself from the crowd. Get creative and differentiate yourself and your company. If you're not constantly seeking ways to stand out from the crowd through creative marketing, you're missing out on enormous opportunities.

• • • • •

Chapter Twelve
THE POWER OF SERVICE

The plain truth in business is that if you don't serve your customers well, you won't have any customers.

As the result of many years of personal experience, here are the things I see as the keys to powerful service: (I call them the "FOUR C's.")

1) Creativity;
2) Consistency;
3) Commitment;
   and,
4) Continuity (Also known as Follow-through.)

CREATIVITY

By creativity, I simply mean doing things a little differently in order to stand out from the pack.

Years ago, I thought that Burger King had the greatest concept ever. They were going up against McDonald's with a simple idea that they highlighted in a clever jingle in their TV commercials. Do you remember this?

"Hold the pickles, hold the lettuce.
Special orders don't upset us.
All we ask is that you let us serve it your way."

"YOUR WAY." What a great concept! What customers don't want it "their way?" What customer says, "Thank you for your offer to let me have it MY way, but I'd prefer to have it YOUR way. And I'd like to pay more for it, too."

Instead, creativity became an essential part of Burger King's customer service program. They may have given up on the concept too early, possibly because the jingle was a little silly. But the idea behind it was solid.

Creativity also means delivering the product in a creative way—creative packaging or a creative delivery system.

I don't know about you, but I prefer my soft drinks to have some fizz in them when I drink them. In the old days, when I bought a Coke or a Pepsi, the fizz started to dissipate when I removed the top or popped the tab on the top of the can. Of course, there was no way to replace the cap or the pull-tab.

Then someone invented screw-top plastic bottles—and now I can hit the road with a fresh soda, reseal it from time to time, and still enjoy some fizz an hour later. Packaging—in this and many other ways—has evolved.

In terms of creative delivery, the drive-through windows at McDonald's, Arby's, Burger King, Starbucks, or even a drug store became an example of creativity in customer service. Fast is often good, right?

One other thing: you must be programmed to sell. And in the way you want to sell… the way that makes you the most comfortable and successful. You must always ask, "What will make it the easiest for people to buy?"

For McDonald's, it is likely the drive-through windows, the simplified menu selection, and the quick ordering and delivery. For you, it will most likely be other things.

<u>CONSISTENCY</u>

What most people don't realize—whether they are employers or team members—is that it's not always the big things that make a difference in the minds of customers. More often than not, it's an ongoing stream of the little things that make people and organizations stand out. It's the smiles, the handshakes, the words of appreciation, and the genuine "thank you" that customers remember.

In the early years of my business, Sheila was the best there ever was at this. There wasn't a package or an invoice that went out that didn't include a personal note of appreciation from her. Sometimes, she simply wrote on the packing slip; other times she wrote a special note and included it in the shipment. She also had the uncanny ability to recognize the telephone voices of our customers before they even identified themselves…and this was with over 1,000 customers, long before Caller ID. She really made every customer feel very special.

I'm glad she was consistent about doing this. Customers notice when the little things change. No matter what service standard you set, make sure that it is consistent and ongoing. The tiniest change can diminish customer loyalty.

Have you ever returned to your favorite store, restaurant, or other favorite place—a national park, campground, or hotel—and discovered that something you loved about it had changed? Your favorite trail is no longer open at your favorite campground, no fitness center at your favorite hotel—it's now a bar instead.

While I don't advocate preserving the unprofitable aspects of any venture, consistency of both what you offer and the customer service you associate with what you offer are vital to your ongoing success.

Think about Burger King again. Years ago, they announced they were dropping the "Whopper," and customers were so upset that BK was forced to bring back this overwhelmingly popular item.

Or consider Coca-Cola. When they introduced "New Coke" and dropped "Old Coke," loyalists went crazy. "Classic Coke" was brought back.

Whether the BK and Coke fiascos were legitimate or whether they were simply elaborate marketing ploys is beside the point. They are demonstrations of the customer's desire for consistency.

COMMITMENT

There are three elements of commitment involved in effective customer service:

• Commitment to training the team.

• Commitment to customer satisfaction.

• Commitment to offering a quality product or service.

A poorly trained team—comprised of people who do not realize how important their roles are—is a formula for failure.

Training the team simply means that you tell every individual WHY they are on the team, WHAT they are expected to do, HOW they are expected to do it, and WHEN they are expected to do it (timeliness, deadlines, expectations). In all four of these key points, specifics are important. There is no room for vagueness. Training really is as simple as that.

Customer satisfaction means that every member of the team does whatever is necessary to make the customer want to become a returning customer. It's what Ken Blanchard and Sheldon Bowles refer to as creating "Raving Fans" in their book of that title.

It's amazing how little it takes to turn a customer into a former customer. Imagine if my investors never made money on any of their investments in El Dorado Holdings. Not only would I never see them again, but I'm sure they'd also tell everyone they knew that they were dissatisfied.

Offering a quality product or service is paramount. But please remember that even if your product or service is top notch, you have to back it up with a competent team and a commitment to customer satisfaction.

CONTINUITY (FOLLOW-THROUGH)

This is a simple principle. If you promise something, you do it. If the message on your voice mail says, "Your call is important to us—leave a message and we'll call back," you call back. If you promise delivery on a certain day by a certain time, you deliver. If you offer a guarantee on your product or service, you meet that obligation. This is what Continuity really is.

There are two key words—the only two words—in the term "Customer Service."

The first word is obviously "customer"—the reason you're in business…and the one whose loyalty and positive word of mouth keeps you in business.

The second word is "service"—your key to earning that loyalty and fostering positive feelings on the part of your customers.

An effective Master Plan for any business involves building a customer base, then giving those customers the continuous level of service that will make them long-term customers.

• • • • •

Chapter Thirteen
THE POWER OF SCALABILITY

"Think Big!"

I believe that these words should apply to every area of life. People who think small, have small ideas, set small goals, and follow small dreams will never achieve big things.

President John F. Kennedy once said, "Those who dare to fail miserably can achieve greatly." He's suggesting that we think big… that we dare to take on bold challenges, realizing that we can fail. My belief is that failing to dream big dreams is the biggest single failure.

They key to "bigness" is the power of scalability. If you have a sound idea backed with a workable plan, there is no reason why you can't take that idea to the next level. And the next. And the next after that.

Think about companies such as McDonald's or Chick-fil-A®. Both are successful in the same field—what they call "quick-service restaurants." (Somehow, that sounds better than "fast food!") I'm going to use Chick-fil-A as my example of choice, because I have a deep appreciation for their values. Their corporate culture is one that rewards employee loyalty and puts faith and family first. They have provided millions of dollars in scholarships to young college students, and they are closed on Sundays so that families can play, worship, and celebrate life together.

Their founder, the late S. Truett Cathy—a man who long held to the importance of all these values—started with one restaurant back in 1946. Mr. Cathy opened his first restaurant, The Dwarf House, across the street from a Ford Motor Company assembly plant in Hapeville, Georgia.

In the early 1960s, he invented the boneless chicken breast sandwich and founded Chick-fil-A, Inc. He pioneered the establishment of restaurants in shopping malls with the opening of the first Chick-fil-A restaurant at a mall in suburban Atlanta in 1967. Since then, Chick-fil-A has steadily grown to become the third-largest quick-service restaurant chain in the United States, with more than 2,363 locations in 41 states and Washington, D.C. Chick-fil-A reported more than $10.46 billion in revenue in 2019, which marks 50 consecutive years of sales growth.

Yes, there are larger chains of "fast food" restaurants—McDonalds's and Starbucks. But these chains—and Chick-fil-A—are perfect examples of scalability. Scalability means there is always room to grow.

Scalability doesn't just apply to restaurants. My good friend, Wes Bates, is in an entirely different industry. His company cleans carpets.

When Wes graduated from college, he had no idea what he really wanted to do. So, he went to work for his father, Jack, who owned a small carpet-cleaning company in Columbus, Ohio. (Wes laughs about it now when he says he was the most highly educated carpet cleaner in Ohio.)

Being technically minded, Wes determined that there could be a better way to clean carpets. He designed and built a 260-pound carpet-cleaning machine on wheels. It could be rolled off a truck and into a home, and the 16 feet of hose attached to it could reach every corner of most houses. When operated by someone who knew the basics of cleaning carpets, it worked wonders.

With the first two machines out in the field, Wes and his dad came to the conclusion that there would be a market for this device.

They built more of them, and Wes went out on the road to sell them to others in the carpet-cleaning business. The price of the unit—back in 1972—was $4,295. Wes earned $1,000 for each machine he sold.

Most weeks, he sold one or two. But the machine caught on, and one week, he sold four…which meant $4,000 in commissions. His dad said, "No way am I paying you that much money." Wes thought, *Why am I breaking my back out on the road to sell these things if I'm not going to be paid?*

Yet, he knew that they had created a virtually indestructible machine that could have a growing market. He convinced his dad that they should form a joint venture and offer franchises.

Wes ran an ad in the Columbus newspaper offering opportunities in Florida. The headline was, "Do we have a deal for you in Florida!" People eager to escape Ohio winters responded, and the truck-mounted machines started moving out the door… on the road to Florida.

Jack wanted to call the growing company "Jack Rabbit Carpet Cleaning," but because of how the machine did what it did, they ultimately settled on "Stanley Steemer."

I'm guessing you've heard of Stanley Steemer. They are a highly respected name in the industry. They have 350 offices around the country, 329 individual franchisees, a fleet of 1,000 trucks, and 2,500 employees. They spend $50 million in television advertising every year, and they have wisely used the Internet to make online booking of their services easy, fast, and dependable.

Stanley Steemer's business plan is very simple: stick with the core business, don't get sidetracked, treat people well—especially customers—and make the people around you successful. In addition, reinvest in the company rather than buying Rolls-Royces and living the grand life.

In short, Stanley Steemer has become a scalable company. They have attracted the attention of several larger companies that want to buy them out, but they have adhered to their principles, defended their franchisees, and refused extremely lucrative offers.

By now, you must be asking, "How do companies—how do ideas—become scalable?"

The Power of Scalability simply means:

- Have a good idea.
- Have an idea that has wide appeal.
- Have an idea that can be profitable.
- Have an idea that can be replicated.

This model worked for Chick-fil-A and Stanley Steemer. It has also worked for such diverse concepts as Victoria's Secret, Red Lobster, Olive Garden, and Chico's, the women's fashion store. (At one time, the principle also worked for Brookstone and The Sharper Image, but things change and stores close.)

In my business of real estate development, the very same principles apply. Here's how it worked in the development of the city of Maricopa:

- Develop land by adding value. (A good idea.)
- Offer a community that is affordable. (Wide appeal.)
- Make a reasonable return on investment. (Be profitable.)

- Create other neighborhoods/communities that follow a similar plan. (Replication.)

We have successfully used the Power of Scalability by replicating our project in Maricopa—with additional neighborhoods modeled after the first one—as well as in Queen Creek, a suburb of Phoenix, and Tucson, a city approximately 100 miles to the southeast of Phoenix.

The Tucson development is known as Cortaro Ranch. Norm McClelland of Shamrock Farms and his family had owned the land in Marana, north of Tucson, for more than five decades.

Unfortunately for any potential developer, Norm had made the mistake of clearing the cattle off the land several years before he called me to ask if I was interested. If he had continued to use the land to raise cattle, I could have easily convinced the neighbors to support anything else, because they would have gotten rid of the smell, the flies, the odor, and the nuisance of having a dairy farm in their back yard.

But he took care of that problem himself, removed the nuisance, and since that time, the neighbors had decided that this was their place to ride horses and dirt bikes. It was their place to go walking. It was their special, personal recreational park. Although it was not public property—it was private property—in their minds, they had laid claim to it.

That made it very difficult to get the neighbors to support anything we had hoped to do in terms of zoning. They felt we were taking away an amenity that had been laid in their laps.

On top of that obstacle, I also quickly discovered that underneath this property was one of the largest known Native American archeological finds in the state of Arizona. In fact, the University of Arizona dubbed this site as "The Dairy Site" because of the dairy farm that had been there for many years. To develop this piece of property, I had to gain the support of the major conservancy groups, the archeological groups, a Native American tribe, and the neighbors who rode their horses on it.

The Tohono O'odham Nation had to be convinced that there were some aspects of a potential development that would be a benefit to them if we were to develop this property. I had discovered from developing the road to Maricopa and working with the Ak-Chin and the Gila River communities that Native American leaders are very open-minded to new ideas. But much like any group I've negotiated with, they have to know what's in it for them and their people.

We found several different ways to benefit them.

Their main concern was that we would maintain their sacred grounds and not desecrate them in any way. So, in developing this property I agreed that any time we were removing dirt of an excess of six inches at a time, or making a cut in the soil, I would have a Tohono O'odham representative on the site for oversight. As we started going through this process, we uncovered some wonderful fire pits and some ancient gathering places, as well as the houses where the previous inhabitants had lived along with evidence as to how they lived.

This was all buried under three to six feet of dust that had been windblown for centuries. Our plan involved setting aside some archeological property that will never be disturbed. It was fenced off and secured in such a way that it would be preserved for all time.

We were very excited, and the University of Arizona archeological department was very excited. We recovered and paid for a lot of archeological finds, as well as for their preservation.

It took several years of negotiations to make certain that the tribe would be satisfied with the way things would be handled, and the city council and the mayor would be happy.

The biggest problem, though, was appeasing the neighbors who had come to know and use this area as "public" recreational facilities. The solution was to set aside additional community property and create parks and riding trails for the existing neighbors as well as for the new residents.

Over time, it all came together because of the Principles of Scalability.

- The good idea was to develop land by adding value.
- Wide appeal was the result of offering home sites in a community that is affordable.
- We met the goal of being profitable, because our investors made a reasonable return on their investment.
- And, of course, we are currently replicating our past success by creating other neighborhoods and communities that follow a similar Master Plan.

The same Principles of Scalability are now coming into play in another large property holding we own near Phoenix. This area is known as Douglas Ranch. There are approximately 38,000 acres (or about 53 square miles) of beautiful undeveloped desert land in this enormous ranch, backing up to the White Tank Mountains.

The Douglas Ranch project is on its way to becoming a reality because we will develop land by adding value, offer a community that is affordable, and make a reasonable (but not excessive) return on investment.

Douglas Ranch will be a "smart city." It will be as environmentally "clean" as possible and will be directly on the corridor of the new Interstate 11, which will link Phoenix and Las Vegas… the first ever Interstate Highway to do that. Thanks to the involvement of Mary Peters, the Secretary of Transportation under President George W. Bush, $100 million in needed land has already been donated to the future right of way.

Though many of the planning steps have already been completed, it could be said that Douglas Ranch is still in the planning stage. But that's important, because, as you will discover in the pages that follow, your vision and planning are vital to creating your Master Plan.

•••••

Chapter Fourteen
THE POWER OF THE MULTIPLE WIN

One of my driving principles is that everyone involved in a relationship, a business transaction, or a partnership should ultimately emerge as a winner. Yes, I believe the "win-win" situation should always be the goal—no matter how lofty or even trite and worn out those words may seem to some readers.

That's not to say that the win-win is easy. It's genuinely hard work, and it requires three things:

- An honest desire to reach a suitable, workable solution;
- An open mind—one that is able to consider a variety of options that were not previously on the table;
- A willingness to compromise—to accept just slightly less than the "ideal" if need be.

The good news is, if you keep these three things in the forefront, you can create the win-win, and, in many instances, the "win-win-win-win"—the multiple win.

I've participated in multiple wins many times during my life and career.

A specific instance with El Dorado Holdings is a deal I put together on the northeast intersection of 84th Street and Shea in Scottsdale, Arizona.

This parcel of land was owned by the Church of the Nazarene, and they wanted to sell. However, the neighbors were a problem. They were all upset about the neighboring Catholic Church that is immediately north of this property. Every time church services were held, cars were parked in the streets for blocks away. People parked in the driveways and in the streets every time the doors at the Catholic Church were open.

As a result, the neighbors had refused to let the church get rezoned to build a new gymnasium for their youth. They withheld their support because of all their animosity toward this church.

Fearing even more constant traffic, the residents also didn't want to see apartment buildings or high-rise office buildings built on the property.

For 15 years, various parties tried to get the land rezoned—and the City of Scottsdale turned down applicants seven or eight times, because the neighbors fought every plan with all of their might.

But I firmly believed that we could do something no one else had succeeded in doing. With that in mind I approached the Church of the Nazarene and asked them, "If I can get it rezoned, will you sell it to me?"

They responded, "Yes, but good luck. Everyone else has been trying for almost two decades."

With their blessing behind me, I laid some important groundwork. I invested months of hard work to create a "win-win-win" for every concerned party.

I had countless neighborhood meetings, block parties, cookouts, and whatever else I could think of—all to draw in the neighbors.

At these get-togethers, I asked, them, "If I can figure out a way to get all the cars off the streets during church services, would you let the church build the gymnasium?" They said, "Yes, we would."

Consequently, I went to see the parish priest, and I outlined my plan. I said, "I want to build an office complex on the land immediately south of you, with a guarantee to you that you can use the parking lots on Sundays, instead of using the neighborhood streets. If you concur with this plan, the neighbors will agree to let you build the gymnasium for your youth program."

The Father got up from his desk and stood in front of me.

"You've been sent by God," he said. "You've been sent here by God, and I can't believe it!"

He gave me such a bear hug that he almost squeezed the air out of me. He was so excited when I showed him the plans that I'd drawn up while I'd been working with the neighbors on the office complex idea. He was immediately on board.

When I believed I was ready, I went to see Don Hadder, the head of planning and zoning for the City of Scottsdale. I said, "Don, I've got a new application here for you. It's the property on the northeast corner of 84th Street and Shea."

He couldn't believe what he was hearing. He said, "Mike, that is the worst piece of property in the whole town to try to rezone. It's in the middle of the most organized neighborhood in our entire city. Don't make my life miserable by telling me you're going to try to do that. We've been through it too many times in my career."

I replied, "Don, I already have signatures here from every neighbor—all of them supporting my plan."

He looked at it and said, "I don't believe it! How in the world did you get them all to go along with you?"

I told him, "I've been working with them for over a year and a half. I've spent $300,000 on architectural fees to develop a concept that all of them could support."

As you may well know, it's difficult to design anything by committee. In this case, I put together a committee of the strongest, most vocal neighbors you could ever imagine. The core of the plan was to build some low-rise professional office buildings. Well, this committee picked out the color palettes, the location of the buildings, the size of the buildings, the way they're shaped, the way they're structured, and they made sure none of the buildings obstructed their views of the McDowell Mountains.

We worked with Mike Davis and his architectural firm to make sure all the neighbors would be happy. I don't know how many hamburger barbecues we had in people's back yards in those 18 months plus, but I walked into the City of Scottsdale with a signed application supported by every neighbor, without exception.

I was invited to come to the church for the groundbreaking ceremony for their new gymnasium. Not only that, but I was also invited up to the pulpit in front of the church, and they gave me a round of applause. This turnaround in a neighborhood gave me a great sense of accomplishment.

Who are all the winners in this "win-win-win?"

I'm one winner, of course, because I got to develop a piece of land that had been sitting dormant for years.

The neighbors won, because they got to have input into what they all ultimately agreed was an outstanding project. Plus, their streets were no longer parking lots on Sundays.

The neighboring Catholic Church won, too. They were not only permitted to build their new gymnasium and youth center, but the parishioners were able to park in a lot across from the church… and not blocks away in a residential neighborhood. I drafted a lifetime lease that allows the parishioners to use the parking lot after-hours and on weekends.

The City of Scottsdale won because of the increased tax revenue these buildings generated.

Every party involved won a huge victory. The priest actually called me an "angel." I'm not, but it sure felt good to bring diverse groups with diverse interests together—and make every one of them a winner! This is the power of the multiple win on display!

•••••

The Early Years

THE EARLY YEARS

*I guess I always knew what
I really wanted to be!*

Mom and Dad in their early married years.

Mom, Dad and me in front of the Navajo Motel.

The Master Plan

The Navajo Motel that my mom owned and managed after my dad's passing and where I grew up.

My cousin, Dick Ingram, me and my best friend, Roy McKay, after a day of fishing (Roswell, NM).

My best friend, Roy McKay and his wife Charlotte back in the day. I set up their first date.

The Early Years

Tufts & Son warehouse, Oklahoma City, OK

Me, as President of Tufts & Son in the Tufts & Son Animal Health Dealer Catalog.

The product that gave me the reputation as the "Number One Rat-Bait Salesperson in America".

Me, John Tufts and James Walsh in a meeting in 1975.

The Master Plan

FAMILY

With Betty Dalton and Sheila during a visit to Oklahoma City to plan the 35th reunion for Tufts & Son.

Sheila and me in 1981 at the Durvet Fall Stockholders Meeting at the Grand Hotel in Mackinac Island, Michigan.

Sheila and me with just a portion of our ever expanding family.

Family

My dear mother, Maude Ingram.

Mom with a few of her closest friends at her 85th birthday party.

The Master Plan

FRIENDS AND ASSOCIATES

Wes Adams and Dave Kingston with me up at the Bell Cross Ranch outside of Great Falls, MT. Wes and Dave were both partners with me in this 8,700-acre Montana wonderland.

With some of my partners in Bell Cross Ranch: (L to R) Dave Kingston, me, Robin Sorensen, Larry Williams, and Shon Craig.

There isn't any time of day that isn't perfect for a ride on the ranch!

Friends and Associates

Wes Adams, Glenn Stearns, Foster Friess, and me cooking some of our catch during our Amazon bass fishing adventure.

Awarding Foster Friess the "Grand Dufus" award along with his personal copy of Fishing for Dummies at the 2008 El Dorado Salmon Fishing Trip in British Columbia, Canada.

The Master Plan

A few of the ladies at the 2011 El Dorado Valentines Day dinner including Didi Foss, Sara O'Meara, Ingrid Poole, Yvonne Fedderson, and Cindy Marlenee.

Zig Ziglar, his wife "the Redhead" Jean, Sheila, and me.

Ray Farley, my lifetime mentor Virgil Haley, and E.J. Bennett

Friends and Associates

With my good friend, Buddy Bennett, in Amarillo, Texas, May, 2012.

Sheila, Red Steagall, Reba McEntire, and me at a Phoenix Celebrity Fight Night Fundraiser where Reba has emceed the event annually since 2005. In its 20-plus-year history, Celebrity Fight Night has raised over $84M for its prime beneficiary, the Muhammad Ali Parkinson Center, as well as numerous other organizations.

The Master Plan

My lifelong friend, Dr. Bill Burch (I call him "Willy"), who brought me to Arizona.

With Tom Brokaw...we are on opposite sides of many current issues, but I still consider him to be a true friend!

Friends and Associates

With Brian Greenspun, President and Publisher of THE LAS VEGAS SUN newspaper. We are good friends who are also often on different sides politically.

Foster Friess with Shirley Dobson and Dr. James Dobson

The Master Plan

With (left to right) Foster Friess and Jerry Colangelo

With our partners, Crystal Hansen and Mark Victor Hansen. Mark is the Co-creator and co-author of the bestselling book series, "CHICKEN SOUP FOR THE SOUL".

Friends and Associates

My long-time friends and partners, Jim and Margaret Little.

Philanthropist John Elway, retired Super Bowl-winning quarterback for the Denver Broncos, and an El Dorado partner.

Dr. James Little, Deb Bricker, me, and Sheila at the 2011 Childhelp Fundraiser in Scottsdale, AZ. Childhelp was founded over 50 years ago by Sara O'Meara and Yvonne Fedderson to protect and help children that are victims of abuse.

The Master Plan

On a 'hunting expidition" with Dr James Dobson, founder of "Focus on the Family".

That's Gary Sinese on the left. Not only is Gary a "star" but he is a true true patriot who is committed to "giving back."

Friends and Associates

The two wonderful women with me are my wife Sheila and Reba McEntire.

(Left to right): Michael Gathers, Dr. Ben Carson, and me. Michael is my friend and favorite driver when I am in Washington DC.

The Master Plan

With Sarah Palin, Governor of Alaska and 2008 Vice Presidential candidate. I count Sarah and her husband, Todd, among my dearest friends and favorite hunting and fishing partners.

I'm guessing that no introcuction is needed. But if you have been stranded on a desert island for several years, Sheila and I are in the middle, and that's President Donald Trump on the left, and Vice President Mike Pence on the right.

(L to R) Vice President Mike Pence, me, Jerry Moyes, and former Vice President Dan Quayle.

Friends and Associates

The larger photo is of my longtime friend, Red Steagall. The small photos represent a typical day on one of my ranches — my favorite places to spend time.

As you read this book, it will become clear to you how much I love America. In order to (hopefully) be remembered by the people I meet, I hand out my business cards in a small envelope that represents our flag. I am also handing out "Silver Bullets" (not real silver) on which my contact information will be engraved. The last item I will pass out is the "Challenge Coin."

The Master Plan

AWARDS AND CEREMONIES

My former partner, Monty Ortman (2nd from the left) with me (on the right) and our architects and contractors on site during construction of our first golf course community, El Dorado Lakes.

Golf Inc.'s magazine presentation for our development of "The Duke at Rancho El Dorado," our first golf course development in Maricopa, Arizona.

Awards and Ceremonies

Audi Redstrom, Elly Penrod, Tom Chambers (the tall one), Vicki Moyes, Jerry Moyes, Monty Ortman, me, and Lon Emerson next to one of Jerry's planes heading to the National Finals Rodeo in Las Vegas.

Sheila and me with Jerry Colangelo alongside the 2001 World Series Championship trophy won that year by the Arizona Diamondbacks.

The Master Plan

The ribbon cutting and ceremonial cake lighting to celebrate the completion of SR347 (Maricopa Road).

Awards and Ceremonies

Presentation received at the official groundbreaking of SR 347 (Maricopa Road) on December 18, 1990.

The Master Plan

The plaque that I was presented at the opening of SR347 (Maricopa Road).

Awards and Ceremonies

A salute from the moon from my dear friend, General Charlie Duke, lunar module pilot of Apollo 16. Charlie was the 10th and youngest of only 12 who have walked on the moon.

Astronaut Wally Schirra, me, and my good friend and idol, Gov. Joe Foss, dove hunting on some of our Maricopa, Arizona property.

The Master Plan

With my wonderful wife, Sheila.

My daily reminder on the dash of my pickup from Dr. Bill Bright asking me the question "Is Jesus your first love?"

THE THIRD KEY: PERSONAL POWER

Chapter Fifteen
THE POWER OF VISION

You may have heard of the old saying—originally from the Bible but often repeated—that "where there is no vision, the people perish." Of course, this saying is open to a lot of interpretation, so rather than head down that theological path, I'm going to create my own paraphrases as they relate to business and life.

"Where there is no vision or plan, the idea perishes."

"Where there is no vision or plan, goals evaporate into nothingness."

"Where there is no vision or plan, the great things that could have happened never materialize."

Visions are usually the result of one of three things: Deed, Need, or Greed.

• <u>Deed</u>: Your vision may materialize because of something you or someone else has done. For example, Dr. Martin Luther King, Jr.'s vision of a nation in which people were judged by the content of their character rather than the color of their skin was the outcome of generations of inequality and oppression. Past deeds dictated, or, rather, inspired, King's vision.

• <u>Need</u>: Your vision could come to life because of something you believe others need. In the 1950s, Dr. Jonas Salk envisioned the need for a vaccine to prevent polio—a dreaded disease. "Seeing" the need is what created his vision and ultimately led to a solution. Through the Salk Vaccine and subsequent drugs, polio has virtually been eradicated from the earth.

• <u>Greed</u>: Individuals are often driven by the desire for more money, more power, or more prestige. Nations can succumb to the lust for domination of other people and other lands. Ultimately, a vision based on greed is doomed to fail. Just look at history for perfect examples of failed greed-inspired visions.

THE ESSENTIAL COMPONENTS OF A VISION

As the result of many years of personal experience, I have concluded that a meaningful vision is comprised of four key elements—or "Master Planning" steps:

1) The Dreaming Stage;
2) The Planning Stage;
3) The Announcing Stage;
4) The Executing Stage.

I remember when our newly elected president, John F. Kennedy, stated his vision for America's space program in his May 25, 1961, speech before a Joint Session of Congress. (I recall the speech perfectly, but I had to look up the date!)

He said, "I believe that this nation should commit itself to achieving the goal, before this decade is out, of landing a man on the moon and returning him safely to the earth."

And it happened! Neil Armstrong and Edwin "Buzz" Aldrin, Jr., on the Apollo 11 mission, were the first humans to land the lunar module on the moon on July 20, 1969.

A total of sixteen have touched their space-suit-clad feet on the surface of the moon—all of them Americans—including my good friend and a great American patriot, General Charlie Duke, the youngest of all the moonwalkers.

(A note to any of you doubters who watched the movie *Capricorn One* and believe that the Apollo program was all a grand hoax: 1) Charlie Duke doesn't lie; and, 2) in 2009, a satellite—NASA's Lunar Reconnaissance Orbiter, returned its first imagery of the Apollo moon landing sites.)

Here's the point: I am virtually certain that President Kennedy didn't move directly to the "Announcing Stage" of this vision without first consulting with numerous engineers and scientists—including the head of NASA—regarding their views of the status of the "Dreaming" and "Planning" stages of the process.

In other words, the President would not have announced the vision had he not first questioned whether the dreaming stage had led to sufficient planning to determine whether or not the vision had a reasonable chance of becoming reality.

The reason people often fail to fulfill their visions is that they process the four essential steps out of order.

JOHNNY MORRIS

My long-time friend, Johnny Morris, is a great example of putting all four components of vision into play.

Johnny developed a passion for bass fishing as a young man and actually fished on the pro circuit for five years. Seeing a need for supplies for this growing sport, Johnny started selling bass plugs along the side of the road on the way to the lake. He got so busy that he convinced his father to allow him to set up shop from an eight-by-eight section in the back of his liquor store in Springfield, MO, the first Bass Pro Shop.

As his little enterprise grew, he was able to stock enough inventory to begin a sales catalog which he distributed to customers in twenty states. Demand was so high, Johnny expanded with stores throughout the Midwest. To further his enterprise, Johnny introduced the industry's first "fish ready" boat, motor, and trailer package—Bass Tracker. His vision also included a massive headquarters store in Springfield, and in 1981, he opened The Outdoor World National Headquarters Showroom as one of the largest retail stores in the world. It was soon Missouri's largest tourist attraction.

With its huge popularity, additional Bass Pro Shops were opened across the country. In 2017, Johnny purchased and merged

Cabela's 82 stores with his own 95 Bass Pro Shop locations, for a total of 177 locations.

Johnny's vision evolved from his love of the outdoors. In 1987, Johnny purchased property on Table Rock Lake which ultimately became Big Cedar Lodge, a 4,600-acre first class nature-based resort and tourist destination. Since then, Johnny has continued to expand his landholdings to include a 10,000-acre nature park and Top of the Rock, a 462-acre incredible property complete with a golf course, four restaurants, nature trail, and much more. I have so enjoyed Johnny's friendship over the years and I look forward to every opportunity we have to hunt and fish together.

Johnny's life story is truly one of vision and also about using his passion of fishing and outdoor life and turning that passion into his vision. I would encourage everyone to examine their passions in life and pursue a vision in alignment with that passion.

At El Dorado Holdings, we are also very deliberate in taking the essential steps one at a time—all in the correct order.

I've already mentioned our current vision is to create a very special Master-Planned community known as Douglas Ranch. I wish I could somehow show you the full scope of what this community will become. But it would take a multitude of Power Point presentations, aerial tours, blueprints, detailed reports, and long meetings to reveal the full scope of the vision.

But let's begin with the essentials: WHERE it is, WHY it needs to be, WHAT the benefits will be, and WHO will benefit from it.

The "where" of Douglas Ranch is about 35 miles west of Sky Harbor Airport, the central hub of the ever-growing Phoenix area. It is beautiful land that backs up to the White Tank Mountains. It is close enough to Phoenix to become a vital part of this vibrant metropolis, yet far enough removed to allow for a ground up, bottom-to-top development of a beautifully planned community. Its location and the availability of abundant land and plentiful resources, combined with a well-designed plan, mean that nothing about it will be accidental or haphazard. The full and complete vision will be realized.

There are several reasons "why" Douglas Ranch will be significant. According to the State of Arizona Department of Administration, Maricopa and Pinal counties are expected to grow by two to five million people between now and 2030. Douglas Ranch is an ideal opportunity to provide an environmentally efficient and sustainable home for Arizona's future residents. Every natural resource can be better utilized in a compact, well-designed, self-sufficient community. In this case, "compact" does not mean a crowded or poorly executed urban disaster. It simply means that an exacting plan will allow for public and recreational land, office and industrial space, and educational and governmental use—all without the unnecessary sprawl of a typical unplanned city.

As to "what" the benefits will be, may I simply suggest that you read on—because there are many. Some of them you could never imagine!

When it comes to "who" the beneficiaries will be, the short answer is "everyone who lives and works there, everyone in the Southwest U.S., and every family building for the future." This vision is driven by need.

Critics question why we are so confident that Douglas Ranch will be a success when other recent Master-Planned developments—all of which are closer to central Phoenix than our planned project—have faced so many struggles. Why do our investors believe in our ability to pull off our plan?

The answer, of course, lies in the vision. There are two primary components of the Douglas Ranch vision.

The **first part of the vision** involves balance. It involves thoughtful design and dedicated land use.

In addition to residential neighborhoods, our Master Plan for Douglas Ranch includes over 7,000 acres set aside for open space, recreation areas, and a magnificent "Central Park" of New York magnitude; land for research facilities and a university campus; public and private schools; manufacturing and distribution centers; and federal, state, and local government buildings.

In other words, there will be jobs for people…and people for jobs. There will be that careful balance—essential to any neighborhood, community, city, county, state, or nation. Douglas Ranch will basically be a "city unto itself," while still being an extension of the Town of Buckeye and a suburb of Phoenix.

On top of all that, there is already support for a new regional airport and light rail service. These are not just dreams—they are part of the vision and the Master Plan.

The **second part of the vision** has to do with the ways in which Douglas Ranch will connect with the rest of the world. In the real estate development world, this is very simply known as "access."

Think about it. There is a reason that cities have historically been built on "oceanfront property," along rivers, and in areas served by railroads and highways. There are not many major developments that are twenty, or thirty, or forty miles from seaports or transportation arteries. Remember, one of the reasons Maricopa became a viable project was because we created the infrastructure—the "Road to Maricopa," AMTRAK rail service, and the development of public utilities. (Plus, of course, the land was affordable, and Interstate 10 wasn't all that far away or inaccessible, especially after State Route 347 was rebuilt as a four-lane divided highway.)

But what about Douglas Ranch?

It's several miles from the segment of I-10 that links Phoenix and Los Angeles. It's nowhere near the Pacific Ocean. And there are no currently operating rail lines or spurs serving this new development.

There's where vision comes in, to complete the picture.

Let's go back in time for just a moment. Up until the 1950s, the cities in our nation were linked by a hodge-podge system of narrow two-lane highways, much like the formerly undeveloped road that led to the tiny outpost known as Maricopa, Arizona. Then, along came President Dwight D. Eisenhower, a great military leader who served America so capably and valiantly during World War II.

As President, he had a vision. It is now known as the Interstate Highway System. You know it as I-10, I-35, I-40, I-90, I-94, I-55, I-75, I-95, I-78, I-88, I-81, I-84…and so on.

But do you realize that there are only two cities in the U.S. with populations of more than one million each that are not connected by an Interstate freeway? Those two cities are Phoenix and Las Vegas—two of the fastest growing metropolitan areas in the United States over the last twenty years.

Supposedly preventing this from happening today is the fact that many areas of fully-developed Phoenix and environs would have to be demolished to make room for the most direct route. That problem would be solved however, by creating a path from I-10 just west of Phoenix, leading through a place called Douglas Ranch, and directly to Las Vegas. This is a "win-win," because we, along with several other private landowners, have agreed to donate the land for the right-of-way, thereby significantly reducing the cost of the project to taxpayers. It's another perfect example of a private-public partnership where everyone comes together. This will create jobs, provide a faster, safer route to Las Vegas, and reduce congestion on other freeways, such as I-17.

This new interstate highway is currently in the planning stage and will likely be known as I-11. The concept of I-11 as a connection between Phoenix and Las Vegas has grown, as many policy makers understand the benefits of a new Interstate Highway in the Intermountain West. This expanded view of I-11 envisions an extension northward to Reno and beyond—to the Pacific Northwest. Congestion will, as a result, be reduced on other Interstate freeways in California. Already, more than 30 counties and communities have indicated their support for this significant project.

Interstate 11 is part of the Master Plan of Douglas Ranch. Obviously, a vision this grand requires a Master Plan. And to execute the plan, we will have to draw several key partners into the many aspects of the program. The federal, state, and county governments all need to buy into the plan.

Thankfully, this is already happening. Interstate 11 is moving closer to reality. Most hurdles and stepping stones necessary to break ground on Douglas Ranch have already been crossed.

The Master Plan

All of us at El Dorado Holdings are very proud of the things we have achieved through many successful partnerships in the past—in the metropolitan Phoenix area, in Tucson, and in Maricopa, among other projects. These partnerships have resulted in the entitlement or development of more than 50,000 single-family home sites, and in excess of a thousand acres of industrial and commercial parcels.

Douglas Ranch will join this list, in part due to the partnership we have formed with the outstanding visionary firm of JDM Partnerships, LLC, headed by Jerry Colangelo, David Eaton, and Mel Shultz. Their numerous past successes include Chase Field (where the Arizona Diamondbacks play ball), Talking Stick Arena formerly known as the U.S. Airways Center (home of the Phoenix Suns), Comerica Theater (a great performing arts center), as well as the Cotton Center, The Wigwam Resort, and Pagosa Lakes & Wyndham Pagosa Hotel. JDM, a firm in which Jerry is a partner, is also owner of the Arizona Biltmore Golf & Country Club.

Jerry Colangelo has an outstanding reputation as a "mover and shaker" in Arizona—as the general manager and eventual owner of the Phoenix Suns, as well as a founding Partner of the Arizona Diamondbacks. Today, he heads up the USA basketball program—the teams that represent the US in the Olympics—and is the Chairman of the Basketball Hall of Fame.

In addition, Jerry has been involved as a board member and advisor for Grand Canyon University since 2009. Under the guidance of President Brian Mueller, brought on in 2008, the University has been transformed from a financially troubled university with a student body of around 1,000 and online students of 12,500, to boasting 20,500 students on campus and an additional 75,000+ online. The grand opening of The Colangelo College of Business was held January 9, 2019. The 150,000 square foot building is the latest of a $12.8B academic infrastructure and technology renovation. A larger-than-life-size statute of Jerry stands at the front of the new facility. The left panel on the statue's base contains a famous quote from Jerry, "The community owes us nothing. We owe the community everything." There is also a tribute: "Jerry Colangelo is a man of integrity and loyalty, dedicated to faith, family and community. A tireless and committed catalyst in the growth of the Phoenix community, he wants to be remembered for one thing—'He cared.'"

Douglas Ranch will soon be the perfect example of the Power of Partnerships as well as the Power of Vision, as it begins, grows, and evolves.

We have dreamed it, we have planned it, we have announced it to the world, and now we are executing it. Vision in action!

• • • • •

Chapter Sixteen

THE POWER OF ENTHUSIASM

I know people who think life is a chore. Work is a chore. Marriage is a chore. Parenting is a chore. Everything for them is a chore.

I don't hang around with them. I avoid seeing and spending time with them. Because, well, yes, being with them is a chore.

I want to associate with enthusiastic people. I want to work with enthusiastic people. And thankfully, I am married to Sheila, an extremely enthusiastic person. This is not just my opinion. Ask anyone who knows her!

People enjoy other people who—whether they are aware of it or not—begin every day with these words on their minds: "I'm awake, I'm alive, and I'm ready for today—no matter what it brings to me!"

Having read this far, you know that I love quotes by thought leaders from our time, as well as from the past. I have several framed quotes on display in my office.

While considering the topic of enthusiasm, I found these, including my favorite from my beloved late friend, Zig:

> *"You can succeed at almost anything for which you have unbridled enthusiasm."*
>
> —Zig Ziglar

And here are a pair of quotes from the creator of the Horatio Alger award:

"If you have zest and enthusiasm, you attract zest and enthusiasm. Life does give back in kind."

—Norman Vincent Peale

"There is a real magic in enthusiasm. It spells the difference between mediocrity and accomplishment."

—Norman Vincent Peale

Here's another great thought:

"Creativity is a natural extension of our enthusiasm."

—Earl Nightingale

And the last one is:

"Success consists of going from failure to failure without loss of enthusiasm."

—Winston Churchill

When someone comes to me wanting to invest in one of my properties—and there are many such people, because they've heard about our successes—I am very careful to make certain that they are enthusiastic about the project itself, rather than simply being enthusiastic about the prospect of making money.

For example, based on the success of Maricopa, there are people who want to invest in Douglas Ranch. Some of them are simply looking for a return on their investment, while others truly believe in what we are doing. It is the second group that adds value to the project, because they will help "sell" it. They will be the ones who will ensure the success of Douglas Ranch.

With all of that in mind, I have given some thought to the "Elements of Enthusiasm"—what enthusiastic people think, believe, feel, and do.

First, *enthusiastic people awaken in the morning with positive thoughts* on their minds and uplifting attitudes in their hearts. They see the sun shining, even if it's cloudy. They envision the day as filled with "good things."

Second, *enthusiastic people reinforce those thoughts and attitudes* through a variety of behaviors and techniques. Some may pursue a "quiet time" involving prayer, meditation, or the reading of scripture or other inspirational words. Others may go for a walk or run, perhaps while listening to upbeat music on their phones. Still others may listen to motivational CDs, podcasts, audio books, or online programs during their commute—instead of the news or political banter. (Yes, I know there are those among you who become overwhelmingly positive while listening to "talk radio." Good for you. To each his or her own!)

Third, ***enthusiastic people are thankful***. They develop what's known as an "attitude of gratitude."

This attitude should not be "situational." It should not simply be the attitude you have when things are going well. My belief is that all of us have something to be grateful for every day, whether we are rich or poor, married or single, employed or jobless, healthy or in need of physical, emotional, or spiritual healing.

Here's one of my favorite quotes from author and teacher Brian Tracy:

"Develop an attitude of gratitude, and give thanks for everything that happens to you, knowing that every step forward is a step toward achieving something bigger and better than your current situation."

If you feel that you have little to be thankful for, I strongly suggest making a list of your blessings—not just in your head, but also on paper. I have actually done this for years, and it has helped me get through the darkest times in my life.

I'm not going to share my entire list with you, because such lists are highly personal, so yours will be different from mine.

But here are some basics to help inspire your first list:

- I am thankful for the people I love and for those people who love me. (I sincerely hope you can include your parents, siblings, spouse, children, and friends on this list.)

- I am thankful that I live in a free country. (I don't know where you live, but I hope you live in freedom, too.)
- I am thankful for the men and women who fought to protect that freedom.
- I am thankful that I was able to achieve the level of education I have—no matter what that level may be. (And I firmly believe that there have been as many great things that happened through those with sixth grade educations as there have been through those with multiple PhDs.)
- I am thankful for books—and my ability to read them. Great ideas live on the pages of great books.
- I am thankful for the people with whom I work—my team, my advisors, my investors, and my customers. (Not many people are all that thankful for their lawyers, brokers or accountants, but I am!)
- Ultimately, I am thankful for life. I'm thankful that I was not viewed as an "inconvenient pregnancy." I'm thankful that I am still in good health. My Jewish friends say, "L'chaim." That literally means "to life," but it is also a toast that means "to your health and well-being." Now that's positive!

Fourth, *spread your enthusiasm to others!* Share it! I'm sure you've been in situations where someone who is depressed and negative can bring everyone else down to his or her level. As Zig has said, "Some people can brighten up a room just by leaving it." Well, the opposite is also true. Enthusiasm is contagious. You can impact the lives of others with your positive attitude. The side benefit to you is that by making others more positive, your own enthusiasm will increase.

Finally, *end your day with gratitude and positive thoughts.* I generally do not watch the news on television at night. There's too much nasty stuff going on in the world. Instead, I affirm my love for my wife, and I end my day by reading something positive (yes, you guessed it… usually the Bible).

I apply the power of enthusiasm on a daily basis, and it works. It's a key element of my Master Plan. My enthusiasm rubs off on my team members at El Dorado Holdings, it rubs off on our investors, and, as I can easily illustrate to you, it even rubs off on people who are initially opposed to our objectives.

Enthusiasm can change the mind and heart of the most stubborn people on earth!

· · · · ·

Chapter Seventeen
THE POWER OF INTEGRITY

Few things in life are more important than an individual's reputation. When I meet new people, I generally know something about them ahead of time, because their reputations have preceded them.

Friends and associates will either say something like, "Watch out for him. He doesn't have a very good reputation." Or, "You can trust her—she really has integrity." I'm guessing that you've heard similar things about people you've met even before you've met them.

The problem is, once people have done something that ruins their reputation, it's almost impossible to get it back. We may try to overlook someone's flawed integrity, but we never totally get over it. It takes a lot of time to build a reputation and become known as a person of integrity, but that can all disappear in an instant. And it's hard to regain.

When I hire someone, I am more interested in their integrity than their skills.

When I establish a relationship with a new investor, I am more attuned to their integrity than I am to how much money they have in the bank.

I have permission to tell the following story as a demonstration of integrity—of doing the right thing at great personal cost.

Glenn Stearns is a good friend of mine who founded Stearns Lending, headquartered in Newport Beach, California. Glenn was a Horatio Alger inductee in 2011. As I have already mentioned, the Horatio Alger Society was created by Dr. Norman Vincent Peale. This prestigious award honors those who have come out of poverty to become successes in life—and have then spread that success to others.

At the age of 14, Glenn got his 16-year-old neighbor girl pregnant. Marriage at 14 and 16 was, and still is, ill-advised, of course, but the girl had the baby, and Glenn had integrity. He worked hard to support the baby all her life. That baby is now the president of one of his companies. Wouldn't it be wonderful if every man who fathered a baby did everything possible to follow through on his obligations?

There are, I believe, certain traits and characteristics that apply to persons of integrity. These three immediately come to mind:

• <u>Truthfulness:</u> What comes out of the mouth of a person of integrity is the truth, lovingly told. Some people believe that truthfulness means sharing every bitter thought and suggestion, no matter how painful they may be. Truthfulness does not mean cruelness. That's why I added "lovingly told." There can always be words of encouragement offered in the midst of words of correction and admonishment.

- <u>Consistency:</u> The person of integrity is not one way one day and another way another day. You never have to fear the unexpected when integrity is operative in a person's life. I can actually predict with nearly 100% accuracy how the people in my business and my life are going to react to certain situations, because I have surrounded myself with people who live lives consistent with their values and beliefs.

- <u>Follow-though:</u> The person of integrity does everything possible to avoid making promises he or she can't keep… and follow through on promises made. When Deb Bricker or Denise Organ or someone else on my staff promises something, I know they will come through—or have a valid reason why they can't.

Naturally, follow-through begins with the commitments one makes. My definition of commitment is: "THE ABILITY TO CARRY OUT A RESOLUTION LONG AFTER THE MOOD IN WHICH IT WAS MADE HAS PASSED". There are a lot of people who have good ideas, but they just don't see them through, they don't stay with it, they don't have the stick-to-it-ness.

There have been so many times when we could have quit because of the obstacles we faced. I think about the road to Maricopa—the story I told you earlier. We were mocked by the press. They called our project "The Road to Nowhere." This reminds me of the so-called "Bridge to Nowhere" in Alaska. It was proposed in Washington, D.C. by a U.S. Senator and a Representative and passed by Congress. Yet my friend, former Alaska Governor Sarah Palin, bore the brunt of the ridicule for this project—heaped on her by the liberal press, out to find fault with her during the 2008 presidential campaigns. Much like Governor Palin faced in her quest for nationwide office, there have been so many times that we were up against all kinds of bizarre odds.

The temptation to abandon an idea that is ridiculed is often overwhelming. But people with ideas… with vision… with goals… are often ridiculed. That's certainly true in the world of land development. It's sure true in Douglas Ranch today.

But I can't quit. There are a lot of people who have put their trust—and their hard-earned money—in El Dorado Holdings. My team and I have to see it through. I have to see it become successful. If I'm asking someone to believe in my ideas, to trust in me, I have to be able to follow through. There is no option to stop.

Over the past 40 years, I am sure many of my team members would say I'm not easy to work with. That may be true, but I believe it's because I expect a lot of myself, and, in turn, I also expect a lot of my team members. A strong work ethic is evident in each and every one of my team members.

People often ask me if a recent trip was business or pleasure. I always respond, "Yes," and refer them to a favorite writing by author James Michener:

> "The Master
> In the art of living
> Draws no distinction between
> His work and his play,
> His labor and his leisure,
> His mind and his body,
> His education and his recreation,
> His love and his religion.
> He hardly knows which is which.
> He simply pursues his vision of excellence
> Through whatever he is doing
> And leaves it to others
> To determine whether he is working or playing.
> To himself he is always doing both."

As you approach your commitments, you have to be prepared to do everything in your power to see them through. Follow-through is at the core of integrity.

Sadly, it seems to me that there are fewer people with integrity than there were when I was growing up. Ethics have been "grayed over." Blurred beyond recognition. The permanent values in life have been sacrificed on the altar of immediate gratification.

The decline in ethical behavior in our culture is one of the primary reasons I threw my support behind the establishment of the Zig Ziglar Center for Ethical Leadership at Southern Nazarene University in Bethany, Oklahoma.

In many respects, the University's connections with Zig go back to the 1980-81 basketball season. Coach Loren Gresham led the team (then Bethany Nazarene) to the NAIA National Championship game, in which they defeated University of Alabama-Huntsville, 86 to 85 in overtime. It was the first-ever NAIA championship game that went into overtime.

Coach Gresham made it his plan to inspire his team to greatness using video recordings of Zig Ziglar's inspiring talks. It appears to me that his plan worked! A small Christian college took home the trophy.

Because I, too, have been inspired by Zig, and because I have a place in my heart for both the school and the State of Oklahoma, I decided to help fund the Zig Ziglar Center for Ethical Leadership—with my own financial contribution, as well as through raising funds from others. (The University's leadership wanted to name the Center after Sheila and me, but we declined, preferring to honor the man who had impacted our lives in immeasurable ways.)

Today, the Center serves new generations of students who will benefit from the ethical lessons I learned as a young man—and they will impact the world with what they have learned.

I believe that ethics—integrity—can and must be passed on to the next generation. Helping make that happen is an important part of my master plan.

MIKE INGRAM'S INTEGRITY FROM A TRUE INSIDER

As you know from reading this book, I have been associated with Mike for many years. As a matter of fact, I was his first employee in El Dorado Holdings, joining him on day two, now more than 30 years ago. My relationship with Mike has evolved from employer, to mentor, to friend, and now I consider him family.

The reason? Mike is everything he says he is—and everything he wants to be. All of the principles in this book are more than theory. They are his first-hand life experience. Over the years, I have watched Mike give back to others, many times when it was least expected.

For example, a few years ago, El Dorado was in the process of buying two pieces of farmland known as "Homestead Village North" and "Homestead Village South" in what is now Maricopa, Arizona. While in the process of putting together a proposal to raise money from our investors for these two properties, Mike received an offer from a homebuilder to purchase the land for tens of millions of dollars more than the purchase price. Closing this deal would have made Mike a very wealthy man. He could have retired instantly, shut down the company, let all of his employees go (including me), and lived the "good life" from that day forward.

But, instead, he moved ahead and offered the deal to our investors, and they received the bulk of the profits instead of Mike and El Dorado.

Mike may have lost millions in this deal, but he gained the trust, dedication, and respect from all of us who admire him. A man of true integrity!

—Deb Bricker

• • • • •

Chapter Eighteen
THE POWER OF FORGIVENESS

Years ago, a great NBA player and a great NBA owner had a huge falling out. Cruel words were spoken by the player. Animosity grew. The player denigrated the owner for trading him to another team, yet the owner remained silent.

The player was Charles Barkley. The owner was Jerry Colangelo. While I know "Sir Charles," and he is a tremendous athlete, Jerry is a good friend and business associate of mine.

In 2004, the relationship between the two men was restored. I can't claim to know why Charles decided to make amends with Jerry. But I recall attending an event during which Jerry was "roasted" by associates and athletes alike. Sir Charles was there, and the beautiful restorative energy between the two men was a testament to the power of forgiveness. This is something to which we all should aspire, and I thank Charles and Jerry for demonstrating it to all of us.

The banner bearing Barkley's number was added to the Ring of Honor at U.S. Airways Center (now Talking Stick Arena), and Charles, who lives in Phoenix, regularly attends Suns games. Mutual forgiveness has made the lives of two men better.

But what happens when the stakes are huge—when the wrongs committed by one party are almost inconceivable?

A friend reminded me of the true story of Corrie ten Boom, and he heard her tell it firsthand. Corrie and her family were watchmakers who lived in Holland during the dark days of the Nazi invasion. Though not Jewish, Corrie, her sister, their father, and several other family members got involved in the "underground," hiding Jewish friends and neighbors in their house until they could be transported to safety.

Their activities quickly caught the attention of the occupying forces, and Corrie and her family were arrested. Corrie and her sister, Betsy, were sent to Ravensbruck Concentration Camp where Betsy died. Corrie was eventually released as the result of a clerical error.

After the war's end, Corrie went on long speaking tours to tell her story. She traveled without incident to several countries around the globe until one day when a man she spotted and instantly recognized walked up to her after a speech and confessed that he was, in fact, one of the German guards who had treated her so despicably in prison.

Corrie was stunned into silence. She had no idea how to respond to this man. Then, without prompting, and with a huge lump in her throat and tears in her eyes, she said three simple words:

"I forgive you." The man broke down and cried uncontrollably.

That kind of forgiveness is difficult… and for many of us, it would be impossible. But I believe Corrie ten Boom firmly believed that forgiveness beats everlasting bitterness every time.

That is nearly beyond human capability, friends.

Yes, forgiveness is important…if not extremely difficult.

I can see four reasons why we should do our best to practice forgiveness:

<u>First</u>, anger eats the angry person alive, while having little effect on the person with whom he or she is angry. I really believe that anger can be a killer. It raises blood pressure, disrupts the digestive system, and impacts the body in many other negative ways. If you don't believe me, ask your doctor or a psychologist.

<u>Second</u>, forgiveness makes a way for a new beginning. I know people who have become "best friends" with people they have forgiven. Old wounds can be healed.

<u>Third</u>, when you forgive someone else, you are taking the "high road." You are not sinking to their level. You can be confident that you have done the right thing.

<u>Finally</u>, you will actually sleep better when you forgive others and let go of the past.

I had the opportunity to erase the past with a man named Ed Jessup. I'm glad I did!

I met Ed during my early years with Tufts & Son of Oklahoma. I had to hire a second salesman, and that guy was Ed.

He is the most natural salesman I've ever met in my life. He has more raw ability and talent for selling than anyone I have ever known.

But he started drinking a lot, which created a lot of drama and mistrust between us, so we parted ways. Years later, I ran into Ed by accident at a service station in West Texas, where he had relocated.

He said, "Mike, if you ever decide to open up an operation in West Texas, please call me. I want to be a part of it. I really enjoyed working with you for the years I lived in Oklahoma. I know we had some tough times when I went through my divorce, but I've remarried. I've come to know the Lord. I've quit drinking and I've married a wonderful Christian girl and my life is completely different. If you ever give me another chance, I won't disappoint you." I listened and I pondered his statements. *Could I believe him?* I wondered. *Could I forgive him?*

At lunch on that same day, I ran into my cousin, Nolan Chandler, who had been one of the top salesmen in the field of animal health in West Texas for more than thirty years. He gave me the same story: "If you ever decide to open up anything here in West Texas, let me know."

It instantly occurred to me that something exciting was coming together!

I called James Walsh, a Merck representative living in Lubbock, Texas, and I said, "James, is there any way I can get you to travel to Amarillo tonight? I have an idea."

James drove to meet me, we had dinner, and I talked about the possibility of starting a new branch, Tufts & Son Western Division, based in Amarillo. I asked him if he would consider becoming the general manager. I told him, "I think we could get Nolan Chandler and Ed Jessup to join with us." He was visibly excited. "My gosh, that would be powerful! They're the top two salesmen in all of West Texas."

The four of us met the next day for breakfast. Everyone thought it was a great idea. I didn't even have to get John Tufts to buy into this—and that amazes me to this day. John had complete confidence in my leadership.

I called him on the way back to Oklahoma City and announced, "John, you won't believe this, but I was delivering some products in West Texas and I ran into Ed Jessup. I also ran into Nolan Chandler, a tremendous salesman. I called James Walsh from Merck and asked him to have dinner with me last night. We all met for breakfast this morning and decided that we'd open a new branch in Amarillo, Texas."

John said, "Mike, that sounds great."

And we were off and running. James Walsh was a great manager. Ed and Nolan put us on the map. James and his new assistant, Sue Buescher, and the two salesmen continued to grow the company, and we eventually opened offices in Clovis, New Mexico, Garden City, Kansas, and Hereford, Texas. I owned it all with John Tufts. As it grew even more, I brought in Roy McKay (whom I had known since third grade in Roswell, New Mexico—we were inseparable growing up) as a third investor with John and me, primarily to have additional operating capital.

But it all began when Ed Jessup approached me and told me his life had changed. I chose to trust him, believe him, and forgive him—and our Master Plan began to evolve and grow. It was the right move. I'm glad I made that decision.

• • • • •

Chapter Nineteen

THE POWER OF PERSISTENCE

"When obstacles arise, you change your direction to reach your goal; you do not change your decision to get there."

—Zig Ziglar

I have always admired people who are persistent in reaching for their goals. Of course, there are obvious examples from our past. One that immediately comes to mind is Thomas Alva Edison. I've heard that he tried more than 2,000 different substances for the filament in the electric light bulb before he found one that worked dependably. I've even heard that he failed 3,000, 5,000, or even 10,000 times in his quest. He wisely said (and I paraphrase here) that every failure brought him one step closer to success. Think about it: Edison didn't change his decision to reach his goal—he simply changed his direction 2,000 (or 3,000, 5,000, or 10,000) times. What persistence!

Winston Churchill's quote also comes to mind: "Never, never, never give up." Churchill had a major role in guiding the U.K. and the free world through World War II, one of the darkest times in history.

JIM WINJUM

Persistence combined with focused passion is a great formula for success. Jim Winjum combined his love for the outdoors with his pursuit of business from an early age. He was born and raised in Great Falls, Montana, one of four children raised by his father, a teamster delivery driver for a local bakery, and a stay at home/part time school lunch cashier mom, Jim grew up in the great outdoors of north central Montana and spent his youth hunting, fishing, hiking and camping. After high school, Jim attended Montana State University graduating with a degree in Mechanical Engineering. Rather than follow in the footsteps of other similar graduates seeking employment in aerospace and aviation, Jim felt drawn to stay in Montana and started his career with a small boot company, Schnee's Boots and Shoes, in Bozeman. At first, Jim and most likely his parents, thought he might have wasted his education, but he knew what he wanted to do and doggedly pursued it. All that engineering knowledge would come into play in a big way later on.

Schnee's was a small company which gave Jim the opportunity to learn every aspect of the business. Jim designed the company's first rubber bottom/leather top "pac" style boot and went on to manage the production and marketing. When the company was ultimately sold, Jim knew he wasn't done so he decided to join with two other partners and start a company of his own...the birth of Kenetrek Boots.

The business was struggling the first several years when Jim and his partners were hit with their biggest challenge, the recession. It was extremely difficult to try to market their new boots when the sporting retail stores were struggling to just keep their doors open. Jim credits his passion for hunting and the "never give up" attitude he gained through those experiences to surviving the tough initial years of this new company. This persistence paid off. Kenetrek was able to grow every year and continues to do so today.

Often learning from his own hunting experiences and the footwear necessary for comfort and stability in rugged country, Kenetrek has consistently improved their boot line. In addition to sportsmen's boots, Kenetrek has answered the call from other professions including the Lineman Extreme boot for lineman and other outdoor workers, Wildland Fire Boot for wild land firefighters, orthopedic and even military footwear. This past year, Kenetrek opened up their first visitor center at their Bozeman headquarters.

Jim remains an avid sportsmen and is grateful his passion for the outdoors led him to a very successful career being able to help others enjoy that same passion.

"Never give up" also reminds me of another good friend of mine, Jane Askew, an inspiring example of persistence.

JANE AND WADE ASKEW

Jane and her husband, Wade, were retired and living in Maricopa, while it was still an unincorporated town of fewer than 500 residents. (At one time, they owned a 200-foot boat—a yacht, actually. They told me that the second-happiest day in their lives was when they bought that huge boat. But the HAPPIEST day was when they sold it.)

When we announced our plan to build the "Road to Nowhere," Jane immediately became one of our most ardent and vocal supporters. It wasn't that she was throwing her support behind our plan to develop residential neighborhoods—she couldn't have cared less about that. It was simply that she thought the two-lane road linking Maricopa with the rest of the world was horribly unsafe. She saw every mile of it as dangerous, so she always hated to travel on it.

Jane became a serious and involved advocate of State Route 347. She scheduled her own neighborhood meetings and attended those held by others. She planned get-togethers over coffee, and she wrote an endless stream of letters to people of position and power. She was one of the most involved and persistent community activists I had ever met. And she did all this from her wheelchair. Nothing could stop her!

Sadly, this story has a very tragic twist. Before the road she campaigned for was ever completed, Jane was killed in a horrific automobile accident on the old, unimproved road. She never lived to witness the outcome of her persistence. How I would have loved to have seen Jane Askew at the ribbon cutting for the road she fought to have built!

We were pleased to honor her memory by naming the new park we built in Maricopa after her. It's called—quite appropriately—Jane Askew Park.

The power of persistence also applies to the story of Valley Christian High School in Chandler, Arizona. And I promise you, this story has an upbeat ending!

Several years ago, I bought 140 acres on Ray Road and 56th Street from an investor in California who was in financial trouble and was losing the property. This parcel was zoned for industrial use, and the city of Chandler had made it very clear to every developer that it would never be rezoned for residential use. But I knew at the time that it would take years and years to develop it as industrial property. So, in the meantime, it would simply sit idle.

ANOTHER WIN-WIN

About that time, some parents of students at Valley Christian High School approached me and asked me to help them find land for a new school. They knew I was in the real estate business and also had a soft spot in my heart for education, so they felt that I would be able to find some reasonably priced land for their new campus.

I immediately thought of the land I was looking at, so I said, "You know, I am purchasing 140 acres at 56th Street and Ray."

They were immediately excited. "That would be a perfect location. But we only need 15 acres."

I thought for a moment and said, "If I can get that property rezoned to residential, I can sell it to homebuilders, and if I can sell it for more than I am paying for it, the excess money I receive will be used to reduce your cost."

I then approached the City of Chandler with my plan. They told us they were not against it. Rather, they were actually *very much* against it. They were extremely opposed. The mayor was opposed to it, the city council was opposed to it, and everyone on the staff was opposed to it.

We began lobbying the city council, and we told them how desperately the school needed this property. I hired a zoning attorney by the name of Paul Gilbert of the firm Beus Gilbert, one of the very best firms in Phoenix.

The Master Plan

On the big night—the night of the zoning hearing—we showed up with nearly 200 parents and most of the students who attended the school. Many of the parents were prominent members of the community, and all of them were Chandler voters!

I had no idea what was going to happen, except that they had put us as the last item on the agenda. To make sure we could keep all of the students and parents there, I continuously ordered pizzas and Pepsi Colas and had it all delivered to the parking lot. Everyone was enjoying the pizza party, so they all hung in there with us.

Finally, just minutes before midnight, it was our turn, and we all marched into the chambers in a quiet, orderly, and respectful manner. It was so packed with parents and students that it was standing room only.

Going into the meeting that night, Paul Gilbert whispered, "Mike, we need to withdraw our case. We are going to go down in flames."

I answered, "Paul, I want to continue."

He said, "Boy, I should have taken on this case by the word instead of by the hour."

I put out my hand, shook his, and said, "You've got a deal, Paul. I'll pay you by the word."

When we were all in the room, representatives of the city got up and made their case. They presented lots of slides, and they gave every reason in the world why this property should not be rezoned to residential. Believe me, it was all stated very eloquently. They were prepared!

When they sat down, the mayor said, "I believe the applicant now will be represented by Mr. Gilbert. He has been asked to make the presentation." He said, "Mr. Gilbert, would you please come to the front of the room?"

As Paul was walking up to the microphone, one of the city council members, Lowell Hudgens, a barber in Chandler, said, "Mr. Mayor, I think everybody here knows the issue. We have all been briefed on it many, many times. Every city council member knows the issues. We have heard from the city. We know their side—they have presented it very well. We know what the applicant wants to do there. I make the motion that we approve the plan, as presented."

Then Jay Tibshraeny, also a council member who later became mayor, said, "I second that motion," and he called for the vote.

I was shocked. The mayor was shocked. "What? There's a motion?" He was visibly annoyed, because he was so opposed to our plan.

At that point, he had no choice in the matter, because the motion had been made and seconded, and the vote was called for. The secretary read the motion, the vote was taken, and our plan passed 5 to 2.

After the meeting, I went up to Paul and said, "I am sure glad we agreed to pay you by the word." Although he had worked very hard on the case, he never said one word during the council session. As a man of his word, he really *didn't* charge one cent for his services.

To this day he still laughs about it. But he told me, "Mike, I paid the price later on. I got beat up for years in the City of Chandler, because they still remember that case and hold me responsible for it."

I told him, "Paul, we thank you for it, and the school thanks you for it. As you know, all of my profit from the sales of the residential land is going to Valley Christian High School, so I know they also really appreciate your hard work on their behalf. I'll make my profit on the ten acres of commercial land I have remaining."

Paul Gilbert is one of the finest zoning attorneys in Arizona, and he remains a very close friend—and a demonstration of the power of persistence.

The take-away here is that it is the union of vision, planning, and persistence that transforms the impossible into reality!

GLENN STEARNS

"Never give up" reminds me of another good friend of mine, Glenn Stearns, who has been an investor of mine for more than a decade. I mentioned him briefly in the chapter on Integrity, but there is more to his remarkable story.

Most people choose to run away from a raging fire, but Glenn chose to run directly into one—with amazingly positive results.

In 1989, with a partner whose family had loaned him $100,000, Glenn founded a mortgage company in California. They were able to grow the company even through tough times. But in 1998, the business really struggled, and Glenn offered his partner an opportunity to buy out his share at a ridiculously low price. Instead, his partner offered to sell his share for the same low price, giving Glenn full ownership.

Then the real estate boom hit, and suddenly, Glenn's company was writing $250 million a month in new business. That success, however, was short-lived. The mortgage market started to crumble, and Glenn began receiving letters from his investors who were becoming increasingly protective of their investments. They wanted Glenn to repurchase the loans.

Glenn said to himself, "Uh-oh! Something is happening here!"

In December of 2006, Glenn immediately tightened his loan guidelines.

In January 2007, he lost 50% of his revenue in loan value, and he got even more conservative. More letters came, with more attempts on the part of lenders to have their loans repurchased.

By September of 2007, Glenn's company had lost 85% of its revenue, and only had $19 million in funding. That sounds like a lot of money, but it isn't when stakeholders in $60 million in loans want their loans repurchased, and another $30 million in assets are trapped in credit lines and can't be sold to anyone. On top of all that, there were numerous class-action suits being filed against him and his company.

It wasn't only Glenn's company facing this drama, though. The "bubble" had burst. The world of lending was collapsing. Glenn was sure his company was going under.

"I need a plan of action," he thought. He decided to connect with a number of mentors.

They advised him, "Don't hide. Address the issues. Approach your creditors and be honest. Talk honestly to banks." Armed with that advice, Glenn went to Wall Street. He went to banks and other lenders to whom he owed money.

He offered them 10 cents on the dollar. The alternative was bankruptcy. To the person…to the company…every one of his creditors said they would work with him. They allowed him to "fight to live."

In the process of fighting, Glenn reduced his huge office from 40,000 square feet to only 8,000 square feet. He tore down one hundred cubicles and asked to have them removed. The truth is, Glenn PAID to have them hauled way. He paid to GIVE them away!

What happened next could be described as "walking into the fire… rather than fleeing the fire." Several of Glenn's largest competitors in the mortgage industry were also going bankrupt. These were well-established offices that had talented people in their stable—people with 10, or 15, or more years of experience. That gave Glenn an idea.

He went to his landlord, and said, "Wait! Let's keep the cubicles!" So then he paid to buy them back. He purchased them a second time! Next, he arranged desks and cubicles in nice, neat rows, and put a computer monitor on each desk—not the actual computers… just the monitors. Just enough to give the impression that the business was poised to take off.

He was now armed with a plan. He went to talk to the office managers of his competitors. "I want to offer jobs to your very best people."

They told him he was crazy. "We're letting everyone go, and we're shutting down. How can you think about hiring in this economy?"

But Glenn was persistent! In fact, he not only reopened his office; he opened other offices wherever he could find top-performing people. He saw this period in time as a once-in-a-lifetime opportunity to find the best team ever.

His strategy included avoiding sub-prime mortgages and sticking only to the conventional market—back to the basics. A week later, those desks were filled.

By November of 2007, Glenn had opened offices in five cities, and in 2008, Glenn's company had its best year since 1989. In 2009, he beat all of 2008 in just a single month.

Stearns Lending grew to be the number one independent mortgage company in the country, writing well over a BILLION dollars of business a month!

Glenn Stearns accomplished this by seizing that once-in-a-lifetime opportunity, focusing on the positives instead of the negatives, and believing in the best people. All that, and maybe an extra helping of persistence!

But Glenn's spirit of persistence not only helped him in business and his financial battles. He was faced with another major battle.

At about the time that Glenn was dealing with major financial issues, his health came into serious play.

Here is Glenn's story in his own words:

In 2011, I was inducted into the Horatio Alger Society. I sold the majority interest in my company right around that time. My life was beyond great. I thought I had made it. On my 50th birthday, my wife threw this big party for me. I believe you were there, Mike. Everyone did a roast. I sat in a little jail cell. Everyone roasted me, but I wasn't feeling well. Here I had what I think was all the money in the world. What could go wrong?

Right after the Horatio Alger event, I was having dinner with Dick Cheney at his house in Virginia: Dick, Lynn, Liz, Mindy, and myself. I said I wasn't feeling well. He said, "I'm feeling great!" He had a new heart. I said, "Man", I don't ..." He advised me, "Well, go see my doctor." So I went into G.W. hospital in Washington *D.C.* and met his doctor. They took me into the hospital, and basically shook me upside down. The next day the doctor said, "We're going to put you under because there's a little something I don't like."

I thought, "Okay, well then go in and *do a biopsy.*" But I *never understood what that meant. It never occurred to me what a biopsy really is. The next day I'm on the* Gurney. Mindy flew home, so I'm by myself. I'm a little nervous to go under, and in walks the doctor. "Yep, just what I thought. It's Squamous Cell Carcinoma."

I remember thinking in my head, "Carcinoma. Carcinoma. That's not a good word." Then he looked me in the eye and he said, "Yeah. Cancer." All of a sudden, my world went straight down this dark little tunnel.

His sensed my feelings and said, "No, no, no. This is curable. There is a 50 to 55 percent cure rate."

Wow. A 50/50 chance of survival. I'm thinking, "That's basically a coin toss."

The only thing I remember thinking about at that moment were my kids. My little kids. I thought, "I just can't leave these kids. I need to be around to imprint. To see them grow. To be a part of their lives." I was just in shock.

So as I laid there, I thought, "All the money in the world now isn't worth my health. It doesn't matter what I have. I'd give it all up."

But I fought the fight. I ended up taking the chemotherapy and radiation. I lost 45 pounds. According to Mindy, I laid a lot of times on the floor. I was in so much pain. I don't remember it at all. I was in a morphine haze. But I got through it and came out the other side.

I saw the world so much differently again. The money, toys—all those kinds of things—didn't matter. My world isn't defined by who I am in a mortgage company. Before that dark day, I was making a lot of money and feeling cocky. I went from 13 billion to 26 billion in sales. We were just killing it.

I felt like I couldn't lose. I was living the high life. When I got cancer, I came out the other side and thought, "Why do I do all this?" So, I sold 70 percent to Blackstone and I bought a huge boat. It was an amazing boat with a helicopter and landing pad.

I took my kids out of school, and I asked my son who was about to go to college if he would forego college. I asked him if he would be a deckhand on my boat.

We went around the world. Before that time in my life, I never sat down for breakfast, lunch, or dinner with my kids. I never did those family things. It was always about slaying the dragons, and it was always about building the company. It was always about climbing a higher mountain. So now, every day, whether we were in Indonesia or whether we were in the Maldives, or Thailand, it didn't matter. We spent each dinner together and it was a wonderful feeling to just share moments with my family.

I went to see my doctor every six months for a checkup. Every time he'd come in to see me at the end of my appointments, he'd say, "Hey, Glenn, how you doing?

Everything looks fine, you're good." He would calm me down and then off I'd go for another six months.

During one of my appointments, I got my scan and blood tests. I was waiting in the doctor's office, but I was actually a little anxious. "I need to move on. I need to go."

I came home at six o'clock and there was a phone call, the doctor. "I need to talk to you." When I finally got ahold of him, he said, "We see something very little on the scan, again." After four years of being cancer free.

You'd think I had learned in life that this is a way that God brings you back to reality…to understand what's important.

I went back in, and they did another scan and another biopsy, and sure enough, it was cancer once again. They decided to cut it out. They had done new work in immunotherapy, so they cut my epiglottis off. I'm in a new place in my life. I'm not sure what I could eat and what I could do anymore. I'm trying and learning. I'm back at it, and thankful again. Being grateful for what's around me. I hope this time it sticks, because I am not planning on being sick anymore.

It's very basic. It's about putting our phones down, being present, being grateful. We need to do things that are going to help our hearts to grow. And we start to realize what is important in our lives is our friends and our family. But it is our relationship with our Maker that is of utmost importance.

•••••

And in 2018, here was Glenn's update on his ongoing battle:

Dear family and friends: The surgery is complete and they feel they were able to get all the cancer out. They are not sure about any lymph nodes that could be impacted, so the little guy in the back of my head continues to pace. With that said, I sat the little guy down and had a talking with him. I told him that life is short for all of us. We need to walk each day as if it were our last. Who knows what the man upstairs has planned for us? We could be hit by a bus, have a meteor fall on our heads, or get cancer. We must live each day with gratitude and be grateful for all that we have in our lives. Surround yourselves with kind and loving people. One day, like today for me, they will all come and put their loving arms around you. It feels wonderful. It feels warm. It feels like I am witnessing my own funeral. I couldn't ask for a better ending. Being able to talk, text, or just listen to the love that we all share for each other makes me realize I did some things right. Thank you all for being such an amazing army of love and support. Whether I last a day or 50 more years, I know I am one of the luckiest people on this earth because I have you in my life. The little guy in my head is pleased. He realizes I am right. No need for worry. No need to feel sad or scared. It will all work out as it is planned. I love you all.

—Glenn

• • • • •

You might think that was the beginning of the end of Glenn's story. But as a true testament to his Never Give Up attitude, Glenn continues to drive himself into the future…In a very big way. He became the star of the Discovery Channel show, *The Undercover Billionaire.* In an Interview with the Business Insider, he shared that he decided to do the show because "life is short and I don't want to have my last breath and have regrets…" And wait…there's more… in my most recent conversations with him, Glenn shared that he has decided to build a new mortgage company.

Am I glad to know Glenn? Yes! Am I grateful for the many significant lessons he has taught me? Absolutely! Do I expect that his Power of Persistence will pay off over the long term? I have NO DOUBT!

Never underestimate the Power of Persistence.

• • • • •

Chapter Twenty

THE POWER OF THINKING BIG

"You will find many big-picture thinkers who aren't leaders, but you will find few leaders who are not big-picture thinkers."
—John C. Maxwell

"No dream is too big. No challenge is too great. Nothing we want for our future is beyond our reach."
—Donald Trump

"Think little goals and expect little achievements. Think big goals and win big success."
—David Joseph Schwartz

"If people aren't calling you crazy, you aren't thinking big enough."
—Richard Branson

"Shoot for the moon. Even if you miss, you'll land among the stars.
—Norman Vincent Peale

"Thinking Big is another way of restating one of my mother's favorite sayings: 'You can do anything they can do—only you must try to do it better!' That's Thinking Big."

—Dr. Ben Carson, *THINK BIG: Unleashing Your Potential for Excellence*

• • • • •

My life has been enriched by the individuals I know who "think big." Not only do they dream big and plan big, but they also become very conscious of how they use their time. They realize that a "goal is a dream with a deadline."

Following are the brief stories of some of the people in my life who have demonstrated that very special "personal power," THE POWER OF THINKING BIG.

• • • • •

JIMMY WALKER

A couple years ago, there was an article about Jimmy Walker in *NEWSWEEK* entitled "The Man Who Schmoozed the World." I couldn't agree more.

Jimmy first started "Fight Night" as an annual fundraising event back in 1994, placing athletes such as Charles Barkley in a mock boxing arena. He had modest success, but several years into this endeavor he decided to change the format from fighting to entertainment. He was also able to entice Muhammad Ali as his spokesperson for the event to promote the Muhammad Ali Parkinson Center at the Barrow Neurological Institute in Phoenix.

Jimmy also brought on legendary music producer David Foster, whom he met at the 1996 Grammy Awards. And added Reba McEntire as its emcee for many years.

To date, Celebrity Fight Night has raised approximately $90 million for charities—the primary recipient being Parkinson disease research.

Jimmy has always thought big, it seems. His philanthropy started way before Celebrity Fight Night. In 1982, he founded a program in his backyard: "Bicycles for Kids." The program has grown into an annual event benefitting inner-city children who, without Jimmy's help, would not be able to afford a bike. In addition to the bike giveaways, they also provide food baskets for the families. Since its inception, the program has given away over 8,000 bicycles to children in need.

In 2007, Jimmy initiated another program: "Never Give Up." Every Monday Jimmy visits 500-600 homeless people at St. Vincent DePaul for breakfast. Jimmy usually brings a business leader or professional athlete with him to provide inspirational words to those in need.

"Keep thinking big, Jimmy! You make the world a better place!"

SARA O'MEARA AND YVONNE FEDDERSON

I would like to introduce you to two absolutely incredible women, Sara O'Meara and Yvonne Fedderson. At one time, they were actresses and the girlfriends of Ricky and David Nelson on *THE ADVENTURES OF OZZIE AND HARRIET*. Since that TV Show, they began their lifelong pursuit of protecting children from child abuse.

After the Ozzie and Harriet show, they were both picked from hundreds of applicants to join Bob Hope on his 1959 USO tours to entertain American troops. During a severe typhoon in Tokyo, they discovered 11 Japanese-American children abandoned and destitute. They took them in and founded "International Orphans" to fund their support by singing and passing the hat among American servicemen.

In the 1960's, they returned to California and instead of pursuing new acting roles, they decided to dedicate their lives to fundraising for orphaned and abused children. Through their fundraising, they were able to build four orphanages in Japan, as well as five orphanages, a hospital, and a school in Vietnam.

During the evacuation of American troops from Vietnam in 1975, they organized and implemented "Operation Baby Lift" to evacuate orphans from the war-torn country. After this, the

First Lady of California, Nancy Reagan, invited the pair to talk publicly about child abuse. From there, in 1976, Sara and Yvonne founded "Children's Village USA" in California. Following its overwhelming success, they launched a national campaign in 1982. That following year, they changed the name from Children's Village USA to Childhelp to focus on international programs for the prevention and treatment of child abuse. . So far, more than 10 million children have been impacted!

That same year, Sara and Yvonne received the US Department of Health and Human Services award. In 1984, they produced and aired the first national telethon. Throughout the years that followed, they have continued to grow Childhelp and have been recipients of hundreds of awards for their service, including ten nominations for the Nobel Peace Prize.

In 2005, they held their first inaugural "Drive the Dream Gala" in conjunction with the Barrett Jackson Car Auction in Scottsdale, Arizona, building this annual gala each spring into one of the premiere fundraisers in Arizona.

Seldom do you come across one, let alone two individuals, who have dedicated their lives to the service of others foregoing their own promising careers.

__FOSTER FRIESS__

Foster Friess is a first-generation college graduate. His mother dropped out of school in the eighth grade to pick cotton in order to save the family farm in Texas. His father dealt in cattle and horses.

Foster was valedictorian, class president, student council president, and captain of the basketball, track, golf, and baseball teams. At the University of Wisconsin, Foster earned a degree in business administration, served as president of his fraternity, was named one of the "ten most outstanding senior men," and won the heart of "Badger Beauty" and Chi Omega president Lynnette Estes, whom he married in 1962. Two sons, two daughters, and fifteen grandchildren followed.

Foster proudly served in the U.S. Army. He trained as an Infantry Platoon Leader and served as an Intelligence Officer for the First Guided Missile Brigade in El Paso, TX. He retired from the reserves as a Captain.

In 1974, Foster and Lynn launched Friess Associates. The firm's flagship, the Brandywine Fund, averaged 20 percent annual gains in the 1990s, causing Forbes magazine to name it one of the decade's top mutual funds. CNBC dubbed Foster one of the "century's great investors."

Foster has devoted significant resources to philanthropy. In 1999, the "Champ" himself awarded Foster the Muhammad Ali

Humanitarian Award, and in 2000, at the National Charity Awards Dinner in Washington, D.C., Foster was named the "Humanitarian of the Year," following in the footsteps of Coretta Scott King, Bob Hope, President George H.W. Bush, and Lady Bird Johnson.

From supporting families of disabled children in Wyoming to assisting victims of Hurricane Katrina and the Haitian earthquake, Lynn and Foster engage in a wide scope of philanthropic activities.

Foster launched *THE DAILY CALLER* with Tucker Carlson and is the largest investor.

After the Parkland school shooting, Foster issued a $2.5 million challenge grant in *USA Today* to fund "Rachel's Challenge" which encourages students to launch a chain reaction of kindness. It was founded by Darrell and Sandy Scott, the parents of the first victim of Columbine. It has averted seven school shootings and more than 500 suicides in the last three years. (More on this later!)

Foster believes that private individuals are called to carry others' burdens–rather than relying on the government to do so. Foster works to promote the Founding Father principles of free enterprise, limited constitutional government, fiscal responsibility, and traditional American values. He believes we can find effective, innovative private sector solutions to many of the problems we face.

After his unsuccessful Wyoming gubernatorial run in 2018, Foster formed "Foster's Outriders." The organization's motto is, "As outriders keep the herd on the right trail, Foster's Outriders commits to keeping the government on the right path." Foster's Outriders are currently working on several projects, including requiring the state of Wyoming to reveal its financial records to the public, providing programs that improve school safety, developing youth mentoring and encouraging a return to civility in schools, and establishing laws requiring all providers of healthcare products and services to publish their prices.

And personally, I believe that Foster's "Big Thinking" will inspire so many others!

•••••

RICHARD J. STEPHENSON

Philanthropist, entrepreneur, global merchant banker, and servant leader, Richard J. Stephenson is the founder and chairman of Cancer Treatment Centers of America® (CTCA). He has been Chairman of the Board since the company's inception in 1988. He is an example of someone who "thought big" to meet significant needs!

Richard was taught by his parents to live a life in accordance with the moral code: "When you see someone who is less well off than yourself, and you are in a unique position to do something about their plight, without harm to self, family or Lord, you simply step into the opportunity and do it." No fuss, no muss, no conversation. Just do it!

Richard is a recipient of the 2017 Horatio Alger Award, which since 1947 has honored the achievements of admirable leaders who have succeeded despite facing adversity, and who are committed to higher education and charitable efforts in their local and global communities.

Following his mother's death from cancer—and the painful reality of her lack of hope-fulfilling options, treatment and care—my friend made a promise to change the face of cancer care: "I never wanted to see another cancer patient suffer the agony of living without hope." Thus, he and his family founded CTCA® in 1988 to fulfill that promise and they introduced to the world what he aptly coined the Mother Standard® of care, the kind of care you would want for your loved one.

During his tenure as Chairman, CTCA has pioneered and proven the importance of a new paradigm in cancer care that empowers patients and their caregivers by providing them with services and programs they desire, where and when they desire them, in one seamless and comprehensive setting. As a result, they are offered more innovative, integrated, and hopeful options with which to better manage their cancer and enjoy a greatly enhanced quality of life.

Today, through its national network of hospitals specializing in the treatment of adult patients with cancer, CTCA offers an integrated approach to care that combines advancements in precision cancer treatment, surgery, radiation, chemotherapy, and immunotherapy—with supportive therapies designed to manage side effects and enhance quality of life both during and after treatment. CTCA also offers a range of clinical trials to reveal new treatment options supported by scientific and investigational research and is rated in national consumer surveys as one of the most admired hospital systems in the U.S..

Prior to founding CTCA, Richard developed a career as a highly successful international merchant banker. He graduated in 1962 from Wabash College and, while earning his J.D. degree from Northwestern University, he established International Capital Investment Company (ICIC), where he still serves as Chairman.

In 1991, he founded Gateway for Cancer Research, which he still chairs and supports and which to date has raised more than $75 million to fund more than 140 cutting-edge clinical trials around the world. This nonprofit organization spends 99 cents of every dollar received from public contributions to fund these trials that have changed the course of life and have brought hope for thousands of cancer patients.

Today, the Stephenson family, including his wife, Dr. Stacie Stephenson, and his five children, are all actively and passionately devoted to his mission.

•••••

HAROLD G. HAMM

I love to talk about—and now be able to write about—Harold Hamm. Harold endured and survived the 1984-1986 recession that hit energy states such as Texas, Oklahoma, and Louisiana. It was difficult to garner public attention to this crisis as the economy on both the east and west coasts was going well. But in the energy states, companies and energy supply companies were going broke every day. Harold was able, through sheer grit and determination, to cut back and weather the storm. He is a true survivor and an amazing American success story.

I believe that Harold is a man who taught himself how to "Think Bigger" at an early age, and he never looked back. Today he is the Chairman and Chief Executive Officer of Continental Resources, and his net worth in 2018 was $18.6 Billion. (There are lots of zeros in that number!)

Here are some highlights of his remarkable career:
- He picked cotton barefoot as a child and started working at a gas station at age 16 to support his family.

- He eventually started his own trucking company hauling water to and from oilfields. Then, in 1971, he took out a loan to drill his first well.
- In the 1990s, he had the vision to use horizontal drilling and hydraulic fracturing in North Dakota's Bakken region, transforming the U.S. oil industry.
- Today, Continental produces more than 200,000 barrels per day, much of it from North Dakota's Bakken formation.
- Fracking pioneer Harold Hamm runs Continental Resources, one of the nation's biggest independent oil companies.
- Harold co-founded and serves as Chairman of the Domestic Energy Producers Alliance (DEPA).

Through his work with DEPA, he is widely recognized as the man who led the charge to lift America's 40-year-old ban on U.S. crude oil exports, a feat that will lower U.S. gasoline prices by up to 13 cents a gallon, create 400,000 American jobs a year, increase GDP by 1%, and ensure America and our allies are never again held hostage by dictatorial regimes.

A national leader in promoting health, education, and energy industry advocacy, Harold has devoted much time and resources to championing a healthy and secure future for all Americans. With the goal of finding a cure for diabetes, he has donated more than $30 million to establish the world-renowned Harold Hamm Diabetes Center at the University of Oklahoma Health Sciences Center.

To further spark the minds of the world's brightest scientists, he established the Harold Hamm International Prize for Biomedical Research in Diabetes, a $250,000 biennial award celebrating the scientific achievements of an outstanding researcher, team of researchers, or research institution.

Harold Hamm has received numerous awards and recognition for his contributions. In 2016, Platts Global Energy Awards honored him with a "Lifetime Achievement Award" for his legacy of leadership, innovation, and commitment to bringing America to energy independence. He was one of 13 corporate and civic leaders across the U.S. to receive the Horatio Alger Award in 2016 for his outstanding leadership and triumph over adversity to achieve success.

• • • • •

JERRY FALWELL, JR.

JERRY FALWELL, JR. is the president of Liberty University, an institution founded by his father, Jerry Falwell, Sr. Both men were gifted with the ability to "Think Big," so I thought you would enjoy this amazing Success Story from the son's perspective.

My dad came from a family of business people who had been in Virginia for generations—and his father was a successful businessman in the 1920s and 1930s.

He met my mom while he was in college. He was studying mechanical engineering because he wanted a profession that required no public speaking. He was scared to death of public speaking. But later, he decided to enroll at Baptist Bible College in Springfield, Missouri.

That's where he learned how to preach and also learned about theology. He came back to Virginia and started a church in Lynchburg. The church grew rapidly because he applied the business principles he had learned from his family, and he started a radio program in the '50s.

Then, in 1956, he started a TV program. By 1971, it was a national television program. Back then there were only three networks. He was on one of them. That built a huge audience, so he decided to start a college. Up until that time, his church had grown by such leaps and bounds, and his TV ministry had grown so fast, he just saw no end to it. But he found out really quick that starting a college wasn't as easy as starting a church and a TV ministry.

Because of all the regulatory agencies and accreditation agencies, it was a nightmare, and we had to go deep into debt to build it. I was just a kid. I traveled with him every chance until I entered high school, and so I was with him every step of the way.

The university grew slowly. It was successful, but it was in a rebuilt temporary metal building because that's all we could afford. We financed the building with a dollar down, dollar a day. All the land where the school was built was bought (a big chunk of it, anyway) from United States Gypsum Company in Chicago.

Dad went up there and talked them into selling a piece of land, 2,000 acres, for $1,200,000. And they said, "Okay, that's much less than what we wanted for it." (The land was right on the edge of town, right next to where his family had settled 100 years before.) He decided to ask, "Well, will you take a down payment? And will you finance the rest for me?" And they asked, "Well, how much down?" He replied, "$10,000." They laughed, but he wrote the check, anyway. He finally talked them into taking $10,000 down, and after he gave them the check, he said, "Now, one more thing. I need you to hold that check until next week, because there won't be enough money in the account to cover it."

They took it anyway! Then he started trying to raise money for the new college, and sold a bunch of bonds, but he didn't know about the Securities and Exchange Commission rules. He was selling bonds in the mail to the people, and the Security Exchange Commission came in and said, "Where's your prospectus?" He asked, "What's a prospectus?" He didn't know what it was.

They made him appoint a board to help him—a board of businessmen to guide the process. By 1977, he had paid off all the bonds and started building on the property where we are now.

We financed it any way we could, from all kinds of church bond companies in Texas and just anybody who would be willing to invest. No regular bank would finance it for him.

But it grew...slowly, and it was all financed for the short term, with high interest rates. It was a day-to-day operation. It was tough.

I went to Liberty from 1980 to 1984, got a good education, and went to the University of Virginia Law School. When I finished, I said, "Dad, I'll come over and work for you a little while." When I got there, I was shocked at how tumultuous it was, how much debt there was, how so much of it was always coming due. I spent the next 20 years working side-by-side with Dad, trying to restructure that debt, reorganize it, and build a business model.

We had to come up with a business model where the college would operate on its own revenues and survive. That's not an easy thing to do.

So, we started the adult education program—VCR tapes with professors giving lectures, along with correspondence materials. It took 20 years to get the Accreditation Agency to say, "Okay, that education is the same quality as what's in the classroom." But 20 years is 2005. That's when everybody started getting high-speed Internet in their homes. We digitized this, put it online, and we were the only non-profit university in the country that could serve the huge adult market of employed people who had been through a year of college, but couldn't finish because of finances. Or they had finished, and they needed a Masters degree to get a promotion. Liberty was the only non-profit school in the country that was set up to serve them with many different academic offerings. We were ten to fifteen years ahead of all the competition.

My dad died suddenly in 2007, but just before he died, he saw that program starting to take root and he saw what it was going do for the school. In the years since he died, we've seen the school grow from nine thousand resident students to sixteen thousand, and from twenty-seven thousand adult online students to almost ninety thousand. We thought the competition was coming rapidly, but they still haven't caught up.

In the years since he died, we've spent a billion dollars on rebuilding the campus and replacing those metal buildings. We've gone on to the highest level of NCAA football. We were already at NCAA division one in nineteen other sports from 1988 on, but we finally made the move up in football. We're one of only six independent colleges at the highest level of the NCAA, including Notre Dame, Brigham Young, and New Mexico State.

That was the goal from the beginning. When the school started, Dad said he wanted us to be competitive with USC, Alabama, and Notre Dame. But everybody thought he was crazy. After all, we were a little small-town college started by a church. But it happened! Not only did we spend a billion on the campus, we put a billion seven away in cash and investments. Our gross assets topped three billion by the end of 2018.

It's a story like no other in higher education. It took Harvard from 1636 to 1965 to build a billion-dollar endowment. It took us from 2007 to 2018 to hit $1.7 billion. It's the first new endowment. We're among the seventy top largest endowments, but the difference in most of those school's endowments and Liberty's is; theirs are restricted by the donors. They can only be used for certain purposes. If they get in trouble, there's only a certain amount of that endowment that they can touch. And they have hundreds of millions in bond debt for capital improvements. We don't have any of those restrictions, and we don't have any of that bond debt.

We offer 520 academic programs and we're getting rid of programs every year that are obsolete and don't lead to jobs. And we're adding programs, such as cybersecurity. We added aviation, because there's such a shortage of pilots. Our aviation school has become one of the largest in the country since we started it in 2004. We are focusing on what programs lead to jobs in a changing market.

Nobody ever thought this level of success would happen with Liberty, the Baptist college that became Liberty University in 1985. It's a success story like none other in higher education.

Yes, it's clearly the power of thinking big!

• • • • •

JOHN ELWAY

Whenever someone speaks of "Thinking Big," persistence or "Giving Back." I think of John Elway. I am so pleased that the legendary Denver Broncos quarterback, John Elway, is not only a good friend, but a great investment partner in El Dorado.

After a very successful college football career at Stanford, John was selected as the first overall pick by the Baltimore Colts in 1983. John did not want to play for the Colts, stating he would be playing baseball instead. John had been picked by the New York Yankees in the second-round draft 1981 and played for the Yankees' short season affiliate Oneonta Yankees the summer of 1982.

Ultimately, there was a trade deal between the Colts and the Denver Broncos, which allowed Elway debuted for the Broncos in the 1983 season opener. Until his retirement in 1999, John led the Broncos to five Super Bowls, winning back to back championships in the 1997 and 1998 season years and ending his career with a record 148 victories. John's jersey was retired in 1999 and that same year he was inducted into the Colorado Sports Hall of Fame. After his football career, John became the co-owner of the Arena Football team Colorado Crush, numerous very successful auto dealerships and two Denver steakhouse restaurants called "Elway's".

In 2011, John returned to the Broncos as general manager and executive vice president of football operations. In his 23 seasons with the franchise—16 as a player and seven as an executive—the Broncos have appeared in seven Super Bowls.

While John is most well-known due to his extensive football achievements, most people wouldn't know how much John gives back to his community and charities.

For his philanthropic contributions to Denver and Colorado, Elway received the Mizel Institute's prestigious Community Enrichment Award in 2017. The Mizel Institute presents this award yearly to deserving individuals who have made outstanding contributions to the community and worked to significantly enhance the lives of others. John has two foundations—the Elway Foundation, formed in 1988, which supports community efforts to stop child abuse, and the Heroes Foundation, which was created to provide support and funding to America's heroes and their families. "Heroes exist everywhere," the foundation website states, and the Heroes Foundation "strives to encourage American pride and assist those heroes, past and present, who contribute to improving society and defending our country's freedoms."

In addition, John supports a long list of charities, including the Buoniconti Fund to Cure Paralysis, Celebrity Fight Night Foundation, Kids Wish Network, Make-A-Wish Foundation, Muhammad Ali Parkinson Center and The Miami Project.

More recently, Elway and his wife, Paige, have devoted time and funding to the Barbara Davis Center for Childhood Diabetes and Boys & Girls Club of Metro Denver.

It's very easy to understand why John received the Horatio Alger award in 2017.

Those close to Elway say he approaches community endeavors with the same mindset and approach that he has for anything, whether it's football or his business partnerships.

"How you do anything is how you do everything, and John Elway is that," former teammate Rod Smith said. "Everywhere he's been—in high school, as an executive in the NFL, one of the top execs in the NFL—he does it one way, and that's the right way."

• • • • •

<u>JOHN MAXWELL AND TOM MULLINS</u>

When I first met Tom Mullins, he was intrigued that El Dorado owned two of John Wayne's former ranches, El Dorado Ranch and Red River Ranch. Tom was a huge fan of John Wayne. It wasn't long before Tom came to Phoenix, and we toured the ranches together. Following that, Tom invited Sheila and me to his church for a special Sunday sermon "Riding for the Brand." When Tom came out, he was decked out in a cowboy hat, jeans, and chaps, with a lariat and saddle slung over this shoulder—almost everything except a six-gun. His message that day, tied in with a message of ministry, was when you sign on with an organization… be loyal and be committed.

Tom started Christ Fellowship in 1984 in his living room with around 40 people, as a small Bible study group. Prior to that, Tom coached football, both high school and college, accumulating 128 victories. Christ Fellowship has grown from Tom's home to being a multi-site megachurch based in Palm Beach Gardens, Florida with eight campuses in South Florida and attendance of more than 26,000 weekly!

The Teaching Pastor for Christ Fellowship is Dr. John C. Maxwell. Some of my favorite memories are when Zig and John would visit me in Phoenix every winter to play a round of golf. During one of these trips, I enticed John to help in the efforts to raise funds for Cornerstone Church's new campus. John was serving as senior pastor at Skyline Church in San Diego so it would be a significant commitment on his part. Using my salesman's skills, I convinced him and with his help, the church was extremely successful in their fund raising.

After that, John left Skyline to pursue a career in writing and speaking. John also went on to start several very successful enterprises including INJOY and EQUIP. INJOY helps churches raise capital and EQUIP is a nonprofit international leadership development organization that has trained more than five million leaders in 180 countries. I've often told John that since I was the one who got him started in this direction with Cornerstone Church, I should get credit for all of his success.

John's books, many on *The New York Times* Best Seller List, have sold over 19 million copies and include <u>THE 21 IRREFUTABLE LAWS OF LEADERSHIP</u>, <u>DEVELOPING THE LEADER WITHIN YOU</u>, and <u>THE 21 INDISPENSABLE QUALITIES OF A LEADER</u>.

• • • • •

Every story I have shared in this chapter is about someone who not only Plays Big but does so in order to make a positive difference in the lives of others. I hope you will find the inspiration and encouragement to Play Bigger as well.

• • • • •

Chapter Twenty-one
THE POWER OF GIVING BACK

Have you ever noticed that there are two kinds of people in the world? There are "givers," and there are "takers."

My personal view is that *takers* believe the world owes them something. Maybe even everything. *Givers* believe that the world (or hard work, education, and persistence) has given them so much that they owe something to the world—to others. Their desire is to give back.

Now, I admit that it's easier for people to give when they are living in "plenty," and more difficult to give when they are living with "little." Financial hardship does make it difficult to think beyond one's immediate needs.

This chapter is about those with plenty who give—and why they do. It's also about how those with fewer resources can also give. The bottom line is, we can all find a way to make a difference in our world.

If you were to meet and talk with a cross-section of successful people, you would likely discover two things. First, for the most part, they are extremely grateful for the success they have achieved. They realize that their success may be partly hard work, and partly being in the right place at the right time. Second, you would discover that they want to give back. They want to help build better communities and a better world.

They all have different and highly personal ways of expressing their philanthropic desires. They may create a foundation or give to causes that seek to cure illnesses. They may feed the hungry or help build facilities that further education. They may give to those organizations that have helped them in the past—Boys and Girls Clubs, The Salvation Army, or the homeless shelter that provided refuge for their mothers and their siblings in a time of great pain and enormous need. (And please note that those people who do not have lots of disposable cash can still give in big ways. Many are involved in donating their time—serving meals to the homeless or becoming a scout leader.)

The fact is, most people do not begin their lives as "rich people." Most of the successful people I know started with nothing. They were part of what has come to be referred to as the "99 percent." Through hard work, perseverance, the guidance of mentors, and, in many cases, faith, they were able to overcome poverty, a lack of education, or other obstacles they faced, to rise to extraordinary success.

As I mentioned previously, the late Dr. Norman Vincent Peale created the Horatio Alger Award.

You probably wouldn't believe the stories of the people who have won this award. They are the children of the unschooled, of drug addicts, of oppressed minority groups. Many had limited formal education. Yet they turned their lives around, and then they gave to others.

Think about Bill Gates of Microsoft. Not the child of drug addicts, but not highly educated, either. He has been called "Harvard's most successful dropout," having left that prestigious institution after just two years. Yet he amassed one of the largest fortunes in American history… and now his goal is to give most of it away.

Think about Bernie Marcus, who founded The Home Depot along with Arthur Blank. Though now retired, he devotes his time and energy to overseeing a foundation that has an outreach that circles the globe. As a gift to Atlanta, the city that gave him his start, he built the now-famous Georgia Aquarium. Countless schoolchildren and families enjoy this amazing destination.

Money has the power to enrich and change lives. It doesn't matter how much money someone makes. What matters is that we all share…that we all give to the needs of others.

I believe that there are basic principles that underlie the concept of giving.

First, **giving isn't based on your wealth**. It's based on your desire to help others. It's your *attitude*, not the *amount*, that matters.

Second, *something* **is better than** *nothing.* You don't have to start big. Giving canned goods to "Stamp out Hunger," the food drive sponsored by the U.S. Post Office, is a good start. Your donation of clothes to Goodwill or a homeless shelter means more to them than you will ever know.

Third, **"Be Happy—even cheerful—about what you are doing** and giving." Don't look at what you are losing…consider what others are gaining. When you realize what you are doing for others, you will "get happy!"

I almost hesitate to tell you about some of the charitable causes that excite me. I don't want you to think that I'm boasting, because I really believe in these organizations and causes.

For example, I am honored to have been involved with a great organization, "Athletes in Action," for almost 20 years. Athletes in Action presents the Bart Starr Award to the NFL player who clearly demonstrates leadership on the field, in the community, and at home.

This award is presented at a special Super Bowl Breakfast each year, held typically on Saturday morning prior to the Sunday Super Bowl game. The award is voted on by NFL players—in other words, peers are casting their vote for the player most distinguished in exemplary leadership. Athletes in Action joins with college, professional, and top amateur athletes and coaches to reach the lives of millions through sports.

Here's a simple example of a way to give… a way that touches lives. This isn't about an actual charity. It's about the "charity of caring."

Many of my investors in El Dorado have been partnering with me since 1987—El Dorado's beginning. Unfortunately, because many of them were in their 50's and 60's at that time, a good many have passed away over the years.

Every time I hear of health problems with one of my investors, my heart goes out to them and their families. After 30 or more years, these people and their families are *my* family. (Some of our investors are now "Third Generation Partners.")

When an investor passes away, I work hard to remain involved with the surviving widow and the family. In many cases, the widow continues to be an El Dorado investor, and, in fact, many of the children continue to invest with us. To this day, I have the grandchildren of some of my original investors as partners!

To honor the wonderful investors we have lost, Sheila and I have hosted an annual Valentine's Day party for those wives who are still with us. We have never wanted them to be alone or lonely on that day, and we want to make sure that they know they have someone who loves them. Usually we host between 20 and 25 each year, and it's a wonderful event.

We typically have a top-notch speaker, good music, good food, and great company. We make sure that every special guest goes home with flowers, chocolates, and a special surprise each year—a gift certificate for Victoria's Secret! Yes, the ladies get a good chuckle and some joy out of that. It somehow makes them feel younger, even though most of them give the gift certificates to their granddaughters! Some of the widows have been coming every year since we initiated this dinner more than 20 years ago.

Several of them have been very blessed and have found another partner to share in their lives, but amazingly, they still want to be included in the Valentine's Day dinner. Naturally, we have invited them to continue to attend, and bring their new spouses!

MORE ABOUT FOSTER FRIESS

I have many very good friends, but perhaps my closest friend is Foster Friess, a native of the small town of Rice Lake, Wisconsin. We're so connected that we talk to each other at least once a week, and I value his counsel and his friendship. In fact, Foster's rise from poverty to success earned him the Horatio Alger award in 2012.

In 1974, after serving our nation as an infantry platoon leader, Foster and his wife founded an investment management firm and managed something known as the Brandywine Fund. As mentioned earlier, after averaging 20% annual gains in the 1990's, *Forbes* magazine named Foster's Brandywine Fund as one of the decade's top performers. This firm has been extremely successful, making Foster and his wife very wealthy. He credits much of his success to his team building abilities, which are amazing.

But he does not keep the money he's made all to himself. He is involved in giving to both faith-based and political causes.

Foster and Lynn are known for their donations and generosity in their local communities providing his hometown school, the Rice Lake High School, a $3.7 million complex including football, baseball, softball, and track fields. However, in addition, The Friess Family Foundation has provided millions of dollars of aid in response to numerous global natural disasters, including the 2004 Indonesian tsunami where Foster sponsored a matching grant program to raise $2 million, and again for the victims of Hurricane Katina raising, more than $4 million, and again after the 2010 Haiti earthquake.

After the Columbine High School massacre, Foster established a $2.5 million matching grant for the "Return to Civility

Fund" through the National Christian Foundation to develop programs to improve school safety, develop youth mentoring and promote a return to civility in the schools.

Here's an interesting example of creativity in giving. To commemorate his 70th birthday, Foster invited approximately 120 couples to tell him, in writing, about their favorite charity and why he should donate to it. He told them he would pick his favorite and write a check for $70,000 to the winner, and ten checks for $7,000 each to the runners-up.

When the time came to announce the winning charity, Foster had everyone open the envelope that they had been given. The winner was to shout out "I got it!" When everyone opened their envelopes, everyone in the room shouted, "I got it!" Foster had surprised everyone by writing checks for $70,000 to all 120 of his guests' charities. If you're doing the math, that works out to approximately $8,400,000! Foster's typical statement when he so unselfishly gives goes somewhat like this: "If this were my money, you wouldn't get a penny, but since it's all God's money, I just love giving it away."

I was very happy to be able to present a check for $70,000 to one of my favorite charities, The Joe Foss Institute, thanks to Foster's generosity. (This kind of story never makes the press, so I hope Foster will let me tell this. If you're reading it, he did.)

Foster is truly one of the brightest, most creative guys I have ever had the opportunity to know. He has very specific ideas in regard to meetings and presentations, many of which I have incorporated over the years. For example, names on name tags need to be large enough to be legible, with the first name larger. They need to be worn high on the lapel. You shouldn't have to look at someone's belly to read their name. Keep any presentation slides legible from the back of the room. Don't crowd too much information on each slide. When hosting dinners, add mirrors with candles. It adds an ambiance and provides facial lighting for your guests. If you have flowers, keep them low so as not to block the view to the people across the table.

But Foster does have another side to him that I have waited to tell because I did not want to adversely affect his nomination for the Horatio Alger Award. Since we are now beyond that, I can't help but share the fact that Foster is one of those people who can mess up a two-car parade. But Foster, being Foster, got back at me after my first edition of *THE MASTER PLAN* by telling everyone he saw that my book was being republished as "Fire Log" material.

For example, in many events that I host with friends and partners, including hunting and fishing trips, I give out trophies for the winners. In fishing, for example, it might be for the biggest salmon or halibut, or the highest poundage caught. In addition, we always have a "pot" that each participant contributes to that is divided among the top three places.

At my ranch, I give an award each year for "Top Hand," and to the winner in mounted shooting, shooting clays, and horseshoes. I also always give out an award for the individual who does the most unintelligent, brainless, or funny deed during the event. The trophy is appropriately called the "Grand Dufus" award. I have lost count of how many of these awards Foster has garnered. (In the photo section, I have included a picture of Foster receiving his 2008 Fishing Dufus award. That same year, his wife Lynn took home a lot of money in the pot as a result of her expertise. Thank goodness God paired them up in life!)

Foster Friess gives more than anyone I have ever met. I think that is wonderful!

But giving back does not always mean writing a check to your favorite cause. It can mean empowering other people to become successful—through mentoring them, investing your time with them, or even providing a loan to help them reach for their dreams.

I am reminded of my 70th birthday when friends surprised me with a wonderful birthday celebration party. During the party, Governor Jan Brewer presented me with a Proclamation designating April 24th (my birthday) as Arizona's official "Pay It Forward Day."

I had heard the story out of Edmonton, Alberta, Canada, where a customer at a Starbucks drive-through had paid for the next customer's coffee, then that person did the same for the person who came right after. That random act of kindness continued for 23 more customers in cars! Numerous countries and states were joining the "Pay It Forward" movement, and I thought it was a great idea. I had talked to Governor Brewer about it, but never did I expect such a wonderful gift.

Later on, after being "roasted" by several friends, including Jerry Colangelo, Foster told the crowd, "I was the guy in the 24th car!"

<u>JERRY MOYES</u>

One of my good friends in business is a man named Jerry Moyes. I refer to Jerry as the "Number One Truck Driver in America," because he started with one truck, and built his company, Swift Transportation Company, Inc., into one of the largest trucking companies in the nation. In 2006, Jerry owned 40% of the stock in the publicly traded Swift, and he was voted out as Chairman and CEO by the Board of Directors.

After that occurred, he worked diligently and meticulously to buy back the company he started. He did and took the company private in 2008. In 2011, Jerry once again took Swift public, but this time keeping 67% of the voting stock.

Swift hauls freight to and from about 30 terminals throughout the US and in Mexico, and currently has a fleet of approximately 18,000 tractors and more than 50-55,000 trailers. Swift is a huge, successful company. In 2017, Swift merged with Knight Transportation. At the time, Knight had over 4,000 tractors and 8,800 trailers. Jerry is the major stockholder of this huge trucking firm which now, combined with Knight, has over 23,000 tractors making it the largest common carrier in the U.S., with 2017 revenues topping $2.4 billion. In addition to his trucking company, Jerry also holds the controlling interest in a very successful steel erector company based in Salt Lake City. Jerry is ranked on the Forbes list as one of the wealthiest businessmen in the U.S.. Jerry's fame is his ability to go from billionaire, to broke, to billionaire—and still maintain his unpretentious character.

Jerry is a humble guy who recalls how he started. He remembers those who have helped him, and he pays them back. One specific case involved a man named Lon Emerson. In fact, Lon was the one who introduced me to Jerry, and Jerry then became an investor in many of our projects.

One day, I met up with Jerry to show him a possible investment, which we called Rio Verde 832. It so happened Lon was also there. Lon was a representative of a large cotton marketing company and had really helped Jerry get started in the trucking business, giving him some of his very first freight hauls.

Jerry appreciated Lon Emerson because back when he was trying to build his business, Lon was an instrumental player.

Jerry said, "You know, Mike, I'm going to take 15% of this investment, and I'm going to put $200,000 of it in Lon's name. If Lon can get approval for his board of directors and from his boss, then this is what I want to do."

Then he turned to Lon. "Lon, this is a loan, so the deal is, I want my $200,000 back, and I want 7 percent interest on it. But you can keep the profits on the investments."

We had owned that property for just over a year when we sold half of it. I told Jerry that I had some checks to deliver. He replied, "That's great. Figure out Lon's cut in this deal but remember there's $ 200,000 there I get back—plus interest."

We had a meeting in Jerry's office, and I handed him his check and said, "Here's your $200,000 plus the interest that Lon owes you."

Next, I turned to Lon. "Lon, the rest of this is yours." I handed him the check, Lon looked at it, and couldn't even speak. The check was for more than $600,000. He was so overcome with emotion he had to leave the room. Jerry was so pleased!

The Master Plan

A few months later, we sold the other half of Rio Verde 832, and Lon's share of that deal was around $400,000. Between these two sales, Lon had made about a million dollars—thanks to the generosity of Jerry Moyes.

A couple months later, our Director of First Impressions called my office phone and said, "Lon Emerson is here to see you."

I said, "Take him to the conference room, and I'll be right there." Now you have to understand Lon is fairly large in stature and can look a bit intimidating.

When I got to the conference room, he started coming after me. I had no idea what was on his mind until he said, "I'm going to kiss you. I'm telling you, I'm just going to kiss you!" He started chasing me around the conference table. I finally convinced Lon that it was Jerry Moyes that he needed to kiss, not me.

We sat down and he said, "I want to show you what I've done. First of all, I have a check here made out to my church. I'm going to use some of the money I made to help build a couple churches in Hungary. And I met with my accountant and we've set aside certain funds on these earnings. I also bought a car for all three of my kids, and I've sent money to my brother and sister so they could buy themselves a car. Plus, I've already written a check to cover my taxes."

But that's not all. I knew that Lon and his wife had lived most of their married life in a simple house that was valued at less than $100,000. Now he was able to treat his wife to a brand-new home—though not the most luxurious house they could have afforded, because Lon is careful with money and has his priorities in order.

With that one deal, Jerry Moyes had completely changed that family's whole financial outlook. Lon Emerson has been an investor on his own with us ever since that day, investing his own money into our partnerships.

This is not an isolated instance, either. Jerry has also made investments with El Dorado for three other individuals in positions similar to Lon's—with great results! One particular investment has already returned more than six-fold Jerry's original investment and still has a portion of the property remaining for future sales.

Jerry shares his success through his very giving heart. Those people who don't understand giving don't understand the powerful impact they can have on the lives of others. And that it is actually fun!

KEVIN JOHNSON

There are countless people across America and around the world who experience the joy that comes from giving time and energy, as well as money. I think of Kevin Johnson, the former all-pro guard for the Phoenix Suns. He gives back in so many ways, not only in Phoenix, but also in many other communities and especially in his hometown of Sacramento, where he was elected mayor. I'm sure you've heard some athletes say, "I'm not a role model." But Kevin really is—in a very positive way.

PINNACLE FORUM

Personally, I enjoy giving in ways that don't always involve money. I was inspired to start an organization in Phoenix called the Pinnacle Forum. The concept is to bring together people of influence in the community to discuss life's most important ethical principles. Note that I said people of "influence," and not people of "affluence." I'm talking about leaders, whether they are in business, agriculture, education, or politics. Having money is not the important thing.

The Pinnacle Forum consists of groups of 8-12 peers who meet regularly in a confidential setting, where the Partners encourage and support each other in learning how to live life most effectively. In the Forums, Partners grow personally and professionally, discover their passions, and become more sensitive to how to contribute to the greater good. They share their experiences, opportunities, and needs, and support and motivate one another—with the ultimate vision of cultural transformation.

I was joined by Jerry Colangelo, Dave Hall, Dave Caven, John Lang, and Merrill Oster to start the first group in Phoenix. Merrill and I had the desire to take the program nationally, and I am delighted to report that there are now about 100 forums being held in 44 cities across the country. For me, Pinnacle Forum is a commitment of my time… and I believe that time can be as purposeful of a way of giving back as money.

There is a wise and long-held belief about "The Use of Money." It involves three basic principles: "Earn all you can, save all you can, and give all you can."

I learned about the importance of giving at a very early age—from my parents as well as from other family members. My mother's brother was a farmer in New Mexico. People who knew him well thought he must be one of the richest men in the state, because every time he ever made any money on anything, he gave it away. He always drove an old car and wore shoes or clothes that were in very poor shape. It didn't matter. He loved people, so in many respects, it was his giving that made him rich. He was one of the happiest people I ever met, and he lived to be about 90 years old—giving to others until the end.

I suppose I could have retired a few years ago, but then I wouldn't be following the advice I heard so many years ago: "Earn all you can, save all you can, give all you can."

One of the joys of giving for me, personally, is to give to other people's passions. Most people you'll come in contact with have a passion for something. It may be for an animal shelter for the care of neglected dogs or horses. It may be for abused children, or for wounded warriors—service men and women who are returning home with injuries that have severely altered their lives.

Whatever someone's passion is, if you help these people in their passion, then they will help you in your passion. It's one way of making good on Zig Ziglar's idea: "You can get everything in life you want, if you help enough other people get what they want."

Apparently, though, I am far too eager to share my passions with my friends—to the point where I may be forced to look for some new friends. Foster Friess told me some time ago that he had sent out applications to replace me as his friend, and several of my other friends, including Larry Williams and Jerry Moyes, have also told me that they cannot be my friends any longer because they cannot afford it. Evidently, I had one too many fundraisers this past year!

My personal belief is that if you're not actively giving back as part of your Master Plan, you're missing out on one of the true joys of life.

REBA McENTIRE

Since I have the extreme pleasure of calling Reba McEntire my friend, I am often asked by others what she is really like. It's difficult to understand how someone that famous can treat everyone like they are her best friends. If I had one word to describe Reba McEntire, it would definitely be "humble." In looking at the definition of humble in Merriam-Webster's Dictionary, you will find: "not proud or haughty: not arrogant or assertive, down-to-earth, modest, unassuming and unpretentious." That is the perfect definition of Reba.

Not only is Reba humble, she is also a tremendous giver to others and has the ability to inspire everyone else to do more. Reba has served as the emcee for the past 13 years for Celebrity Fight Night in Phoenix, an annual star-studded charity event that has provided approximately $90 million to numerous charities with Barrow Neurological Foundation its prime recipient.

Her warmth and hospitality make everyone present pull out their wallets. When she was presented with the Andrea Bocelli Foundation Humanitarian Award at the 20th annual Celebrity Fight Night event in Italy, she described her charitable work by saying, "To know that you can lend a hand and make someone's life a little better brings you back up to realize why you are on this earth in the first place and that's to learn how you can grow as a better person by giving and loving…." Reba was very deservingly inducted into the Horatio Alger Society in 2018.

BOYSIE BOLLINGER

This is one last story on THE POWER OF GIVING BACK… (Last, but certainly not least.)

It's one thing to THINK BIG (and dream big) but is entirely another thing to ACT BIG…to carry out those thoughts and dreams in powerful ways—by GIVING BACK!

My friend, Donald T. "Boysie" Bollinger, is someone who was able to "connect the dots" and transform his big thoughts and dreams into reality! As a result, he was able to GIVE BIG. That's one of his traits that makes me so proud and pleased to call him my friend.

Boysie's father was a machinist in a shipyard when World War II (WWII) ended. When the owner died, dad went to New Orleans and bought a WWII surplus machine shop, moved it to the banks of Bayou Lafourche and opened up his own machine shop. He later moved the shop to Lockport and built the family house in the middle of the shipyard. So, Boysie literally grew up in the company.

The original shipyard was small, so his father started working with his brothers to develop sideline businesses. They ventured into the offshore oil industry by towing the oil from the rigs with a barge and tug because, at that time, there were no pipelines. They then expanded into the supply business where they serviced the rigs.

When Boysie finished college, he went to work at the shipyard. No coat and tie: his business suit was boots and jeans. In 1984, when oil went from $40/barrel to $8/barrel, all of their businesses suffered. So Boysie decided they needed to determine what business they were going to be in. He became aggressive and obtained a government contract to build some patrol boats. After securing that contract, the other subsidiary businesses were sold, and the shipyard grew due to that Coast Guard contract. The company has built every Coast Guard patrol boat since 1984—approximately 160 boats.

Since they were building boats bigger than they could repair, Boysie opened up a second shipyard which later expanded to 14 shipyards in Louisiana and Texas, thereby becoming the largest non-pure government shipyard in America. Boysie credits the company's success to dedication and hard work. According to Boysie, "We've had a great running business. In the early years, all of my customers were friends which was a wonderful position to be in because we did things together as friends and as business relationship. I'm a strong believer in relationships. I don't need to be in business with people who are not honest, and I surely don't want to be in business with people I don't know and don't agree with… as people we should never forget that relationships are important."

When Boysie first came out to Arizona to look at El Dorado's real estate investment opportunities he told me, "I wanted to see who you were more than I wanted to see what the real estate was. And the more I saw the people around you and how you operate, the more I was glad to be investing with you. It's not about money, it's about building something together." I couldn't agree more.

When his "ship came in," Boysie turned that ship's cargo into major gifts for others.

And I really mean, real ships!

Boysie is Chairman and Chief Executive Officer of Bollinger Shipyards, Inc., the family-owned business established in 1946. Bollinger's is a full-service marine construction and ship repair company headquartered in Lockport, Louisiana with 10 divisions in Louisiana and another one in Texas.

But Boysie is involved FAR BEYOND the shipyard! He truly gives back! Boysie told me his father taught him that he had to give back. And not just in resources, but in time and in service. He encouraged the kids to be involved in service work, as well as in their careers. "It made a huge difference in my life. Number one,

I think it developed my leadership skills. I've been involved with probably 30 to 40 organizations, all of which I've chaired." He told me he goes in without an objective, except to do good for the group.

Boysie serves on numerous Boards of Directors, including Chairman of the Board of First Bank and Trust, as well as on the Board of Directors of the Signal Mutual Indemnity Association and the University Medical Center Management Corporation.

Additionally, he devotes considerable time to professional and civic organizations. He serves on more boards and has received more awards than about anyone I know.

Boysie currently serves on the National Petroleum Council. He previously served on the President's Export Council under the administration of President George H. W. Bush. He is past Chairman of the Governor's Maritime Advisory Task Force, and on the board of the Governor's Advisory Commission on Military Affairs. Boysie was also chosen as a "Louisiana Legend" by Louisiana Public Broadcasting. Yes, his "Trophy Room" is bursting with awards! He deserves them!

But in my opinion, Boysie Bollinger's greatest single achievement is his involvement with—and financial support of—The National World War II Museum in New Orleans. He realizes that the "greatest generation," as Tom Brokaw referred to them in his bestselling book with that title, deserves to be honored through a first-class "destination" museum. For that reason, he is the museum's largest contributor, and he is funding a magnificent new feature at the Museum. Ground was broken in 2018 for what museum officials believe will become an iconic landmark—not only for the museum's campus, but also for the entire city of New Orleans. It is called the "Bollinger Canopy of Peace," and from what I've seen, it will be both magnificent and stunning!

This museum should definitely be on your "bucket list." When Boysie talks about the museum he says, "The one thing that I'm really hoping is that the museum continues to tell the story for our young people, so they don't lose sight of the price that has been paid by those who've gone before us and those that have fought for our freedoms. It's so easy for us to take it for granted."

Boysie Bollinger is a remarkable example of a simple truth: "When your ship comes in and you are financially empowered, it's your responsibility to send other ships back on the seas, to deliver boundless treasures to other people and other significant causes." That "giving back" has long been his primary vision and he has been doing it for decades. Here is my favorite "quote" from my recent extended interview with Boysie: "You don't really need to have a long-range plan. But what you really DO need is a long-range vision."

• • • • •

Chapter Twenty-two
THE POWER OF FREEDOM

I love America, and I love the freedom and opportunity our country offers to all of us! If you somehow haven't noticed my personal bias by now, this is your reminder.

Overall, the world is a wonderful place, despite the wars that need to be ended, the suffering that is begging to be healed, the illnesses that demand cures, and the spiritual needs that must be addressed. There are nations around the world that offer opportunities for people of all races, creeds, and socio-economic backgrounds to create better lives for themselves. But none compares with the United States of America.

In fact, when I meet new business prospects and potential partners, I choose to make it known that I love our country, that I am a patriot, and I am not ashamed of that fact. That's why I enclose my business cards in small envelopes that bear our flag—the Stars and Stripes. The people to whom I hand this tend to remember it, too—in a positive way.

I recently decided to add an extra element for those times when I want to make an impression and be remembered. Maybe it's due to my love of the "Lone Ranger" from my youth or simply due to my marketing background. I am designing a silver bullet (not real silver) engraved with my name and business. If you are old enough, you may recall the Lone Ranger used silver bullets as his calling card. In the TV series, the Lone Ranger would always leave a silver bullet when he left. The line I remember was "Who was that masked man…I don't know but he left a silver bullet." They were meant as a symbol of justice and a reminder that life, like silver, has value and is not to be wasted or thrown away.

I have included a picture of my card and the envelope along with the "silver" bullet and my Challenge Coin (which I will discuss later) in the photo section of this book.

Remember, I basically started with nothing. My dad died when I was thirteen years old, and I worked alongside my mom to keep our small New Mexico motel from the grip of foreclosure. Years later, I had a successful business that was on the edge of failure and I couldn't find a bank that would loan me a dime, so I sold everything for pennies on the dollar. I moved to Arizona in a rented U-Haul truck and rebuilt my life with my wife Sheila at my side.

I love the United States of America!

What makes our nation so special is the opportunity it offers to everyone, regardless of the situations into which we were born.

And what turns those opportunities into positive realities are the values we hold so close to our hearts. I've shared my thoughts on so many of those values in the pages of this book: integrity, teamwork, trust, loyalty, forgiveness, and persistence, among others.

Personally, I am inspired to do my part to help make America a better nation—and our world better for all—by passing these values to the next generation. I believe that all of us who live in a free society, no matter where it is in the world, have a responsibility to do everything we can to promote and protect our values. Paul Harvey, the great news commentator, put it this way: "For me, success is to leave the woodpile a little higher than I found it."

Unless you grew up "rural," you may not know what this expression means. In the "olden days," people who were traveling across the country would come across unoccupied cabins that were open to visitors. The owners would leave the doors unlocked so that weary travelers could find rest and shelter. Of course, there would be a stack of wood outside so that the travelers could build a warm fire in the fireplace or stove.

In that time, no considerate traveler would ever burn all the wood without chopping more wood and replacing the logs and kindling they had taken from the woodpile.

That's an example of what we must do as a society. That's what we need to do as a country. We have to leave the woodpile just a little higher than it was when we inherited it.

If we don't, our kids, our grandkids, and generations coming after them are going to be faced with major problems. We're burning the wood. We are burning it at an unbelievable rate.

Many people are truly concerned about leaving the woodpile higher than they found it. Our men and women of the armed services are truly doing it. Not only are they defending our freedoms, but they also contribute to humanitarian causes in the lands they defend. There are lots of great stories about the humanitarian acts performed by our people in uniform.

The men and women of our military today have joined the legions of Americans who fought in the Revolutionary War, as well as in all the wars that came after that—including World War I, World War II, Korea, Vietnam, and the War on Terrorism. There was a tremendous price paid by so many heroes. All of these wars involved great sacrifice, and it is that sacrifice that has defended one of the greatest democracies that's ever been formed—against enemies both foreign and domestic.

In my travels I have encountered active servicemen and veterans, and on occasion I have been given what is referred to as a "Challenge Coin." I've always been very honored to receive them. I've recently selected a challenge coin of my own to be able to share with others. One side of the coin states "Land of the Free Because of the Brave." The other side, "Honoring those who Protect our Freedom. We Stand for The Flag."

Today, I believe we have enemies within that are slowly but systematically destroying our freedoms. These enemies tell us that we are not a great nation. They tell us that we are seriously flawed. They tell us that our foundational documents—the Constitution and the Bill of Rights—need revision, or even dismantling. They tell us that the flag and the Pledge of Allegiance are worn out vestiges of another time.

I want to fight that trend. That's why I'm involved with the Joe Foss Institute. You may have never heard of it before now, but the Joe Foss Institute is committed to protecting the Constitution and the Bill of Rights by teaching these essential principles to the next generation.

I met Joe many years ago, and in my mind, he was a real-life John Wayne. He was bigger than life.

Joe was born and raised on a farm in South Dakota. When World War II broke out, Joe enlisted. He became one of the most decorated airmen in the war, shooting down 26 Japanese warplanes. For that, he was awarded the Congressional Medal of Honor—the highest award given for military valor.

Joe returned to South Dakota after the war ended, and became, among other things, a state legislator. When the Korean War began, Joe decided he wanted to serve again. But he was told he was too old and that he was already a hero, so he didn't need to serve again. Joe would have no part of that talk, so he joined the Air Force. He retired from military life as a General in the Air Force and a Captain in the Marines.

In retrospect, Joe had a powerful perspective on his passion to serve his country. He said, *"Those of us who lived have to represent those who didn't make it."*

Sometime after his return to South Dakota, he was elected the State's Governor and termed out after two terms in office. Then he took on the position as the Commissioner of the American Football League, which was a new league created to take on the supremacy of the NFL. Joe challenged the legendary Pete Roselle to set up a game pitting the AFL champion against the NFL champion. Pete finally yielded to the idea, if only to demonstrate to Joe that the two leagues weren't anywhere close to the same level. But in the third year, Joe's AFL team, the New York Jets, led by quarterback Joe Namath, won the game. And that, football fans, led to the creation of the Super Bowl and the merger of NFL with AFL.

Joe was also something of a television star, first hosting ABC television's *The American Sportsman* from 1964 to 1967, and then hosting and producing his own syndicated series, *The Outdoorsman: Joe Foss*, which ran from 1967 to 1974. In 1988, being the true outdoor sportsman he was, Joe was elected President of the National Rifle Association. (If you're interested, you can read about

Joe's life in the book, *A PROUD AMERICAN: The Autobiography of Joe Foss*, written by Joe and his wife, Didi. His is a fascinating and inspiring story.)

I have learned several significant things from Joe. He often said, "When I was Governor and later on as Commissioner of the AFL, people would come to me and tell me, 'We have a problem.' I would stop them in their tracks. I would ask them, 'Is this life threatening to me or to one of my family members?' They would say, 'Well, no, but we have a problem.' I would respond, 'No, Sir, we don't. I know what a problem is. I've been shot down behind enemy lines three times, and I have stared down the barrel of a gun in enemy hands. I know what a problem is. What you are talking about is a situation that has to be dealt with. It is not a problem.'"

Joe was witty, smart, incisive, and decisive. Four great qualities in any individual, I believe.

I also believe that the one thing that Joe will be most remembered for is the creation of the Joe Foss Institute, co-founded with his wife, Didi. Their basic idea was: "We must educate the youth of our nation about the principles of freedom." If you go back in history, he based that idea on a similar statement by John Adams, one of our nation's founders.

Joe said that Ronald Reagan had it right when he made the statement that we were just one generation away from losing our democracy. He continued to paraphrase President Reagan, saying that kids do not understand it, and they don't pick it up through osmosis or through heredity, so we must educate the next generation about the price that has been paid for the freedoms we all enjoy today.

Joe's concept was to enlist veterans—he called them VIPs or Veterans Inspiring Patriotism—to help educate young people about our freedoms. Today, volunteer veterans serve in more than 40 states, going into schools every year to teach the principles of democracy. They talk about the price they, and their comrades who never returned from the battlefield, paid to defend freedom. The goal is to present the program in every school in every state in the United States.

The Joe Foss Institute has a great Advisory Board of Directors in place. It includes Tom Brokaw, author of *THE GREATEST GENERATION* and *THE TIME OF OUR LIVES*, Colonel Oliver North, former Vice President Dan Quayle, football great John Elway, and many other distinguished Americans. Formerly, I served as Vice-Chairman of the board, and was truly honored to be involved.

The Institute recently initiated a new program called E-Citizenship. This is a collaborative effort between the Institute and educators around the country. The objective is to develop a lesson plan that can easily be implemented, all at no cost to the school district.

Arizona has taken the lead in the nation by passing a law requiring that every classroom in the state must prominently display the American flag, and every classroom from 7th grade to the 12th grade must have the Constitution and the Bill of Rights prominently displayed.

Naturally, some teachers objected. There's always someone who has some strange reason why something like this shouldn't be done. Other educators said, "Well, it's great that the legislature passed that law, but they didn't fund it."

We offered a solution. We said, "We'll bring you into compliance. Let us come to your school and make presentations and place our curriculum in your classes, and we'll provide the flags and the copies of the Constitution and the Bill of Rights." They loved the idea!

Today, the Institute is going state by state asking each to enact legislation requiring high school students to pass the same test that every immigrant must pass for citizenship into the United Sates.

The Joe Foss Institute is very important to me, because my freedom is very important to me. I am very much a patriot. I grew up saying the Pledge of Allegiance in school every day, and I think it's sad that we've gotten away from that. I am pleased, however, that so many Americans have "Support our Troops" ribbons on their cars. I have never served in the armed services, but I really want to honor those who have sacrificed so much. Bravery, valor, and patriotism are so underrated.

Every time I see a young serviceman or woman who is missing a leg or an arm or an eye, I think to myself, "A Purple Heart is nowhere near enough of a 'thank you' for what they have given for the cause of Freedom."

May I make a simple suggestion? If you are in the position within your organization where you do hiring or can influence the hiring policies, please make a place in your heart or on your team for a returning veteran.

I know you've heard it before, but with freedom comes responsibility. I believe my responsibility is to leave the woodpile a little higher than I found it—and to me, part of that means that I have to do everything possible to preserve and protect our freedoms by passing the values that shaped America on to the next generation. Please join me: www.joefoss.com.

• • • • •

IN SUMMARY
THE ULTIMATE MASTER PLAN

Here is the Bottom Line: despite my successes—and, yes, my failures—I am simply the product of "Small Town America." I was that kid who struggled to get acceptable grades in school. I was that kid who was also chosen last for every sandlot ballgame.

But I was also the kid whose parents, while I was very young, taught me a beautiful, simple truth: WE LOVE YOU! I knew that, of course, but it took many years and many ups and downs (with some of the downs leading me to despair), to fully accept those words as absolute truth. When I was in the midst of shutting down my companies in Oklahoma, I had serious doubts. I wasn't sure that I was loved.

After all, I had a CFO who had embezzled money, salesmen who fought the sale, and a greedy attorney who tried to get far more than his fair share. I was let down by many people I had known and trusted for years. And the banks, of course, had been no help. Did I feel loved by anyone? No, not really.

There were so many times when I could feel the darkness closing in on me, and questions would tumble through my mind. "How am I going to survive? How in the world am I going to pay the bills? How am I going to make it through this darkness?"

The Master Plan

During that time, I'd ask Sheila to let me leave the bathroom light on at night. Even though she likes it pitch black when she's sleeping, she understood and she was gracious. She knew I needed to see some ray of light.

I think there are a lot of people in this world who need to see a glimmer of hope—of light. There are people who are hurting so bad because they believe they don't have hope. I found myself in that situation. I thought long and hard every night in the dark—except for a little bit of light shining from the bathroom. To this day, I still leave the light on in the bathroom. It's become a habit—I like to see a light on.

The one good thing that happened during that dark time when I was forced to sell my business is that Sheila and I decided to take the trip to Hong Kong that we had won from one of our suppliers. We had earned it, and we believed it could be a good thing for us mentally and emotionally.

We flew from Oklahoma City to Seattle, where we stayed overnight at a Howard Johnson's before the long flight to Hong Kong. There was a dinner party for all the other winners that night, but I didn't feel like a party. Sheila went alone.

While she was out, I stayed in the room and felt sorry for myself. In fact, I don't believe I've ever sunk so low in depression and despair than I did that night.

But then, unexpectedly, things started turning around in my heart. I decided to turn on the TV to get my mind off my situation. It worked! It happened to be Labor Day weekend, and the Jerry Lewis Telethon to benefit Muscular Dystrophy was what came on the screen. I didn't change the channel—even though a John Wayne western would have suited me just fine right then. I watched Jerry and his "kids." These kids were fighting huge odds against a disease that had paralyzed them.

I thought, "What am I even thinking? These kids will face so much for the rest of their lives. And their lives will probably be shortened by their illness. Here I sit, healthy and whole, and I'm depressed about my current situation. I'm lost in self-pity and there is no excuse for it."

My "lessons in life" continued when Sheila got back to the room. She was carrying a book that she had bought for me. It was THE BE-HAPPY ATTITUDES by Dr. Robert Schuller.

My attitude began changing that night. I started reading Dr. Schuller's book in the room, and I finished it the next day on the plane. I realized that a positive attitude had to rule my life.

I realized something more that night. Life is not about doing good things for others. It's not about money or investments or even giving. And while our relationships are extremely important, it's not even about that.

Life is about discovering the Master Plan for me… for you… for us. With a lump in my throat, I had to seriously think and evaluate his question and my answer. I also decided I needed to change that.

Ultimately, life is not all about me. It's about others. THAT is THE Master Plan.

• • • • •

AFTERWORD

A SPECIAL P.S. TO EVERY READER AND EVERY FRIEND:

It is my hope that, in reading this book, you found something that might inspire you and help you in formulating your own Master Plan.

I would like to leave you with this final thought. Back in the early days of cattle ranches, every rancher had a unique brand to mark his or her herd, to distinguish it from any others. Cowboys who hired on and rode for the brand signaled that they were committed and loyal to that rancher. "Ride for the brand," in the words of the western writer, Louis L'Amour, was an expression of loyalty to a man's employer or the particular outfit he rode for. It was considered a compliment of the highest order in an almost feudal society. If a man did not like a ranch or the way the rancher conducted affairs, he was free to quit—and many did. But if he stayed on, he gave his loyalty and expected to do nothing less.

In everything you do, whether in your business, your career, your family, or your faith: Commit, Be Loyal, and Ride for the Brand.

Here is a quote from a poem by Red Steagall: "Ride for the Brand."

"Son, a man's brand is his own special mark that says this is mine, leave it alone. You hire out to a man, ride for his brand and protect it like it was your own."

—Mike Ingram

ACKNOWLEDGMENTS

Most authors acknowledge the people they love, followed by the people who contributed to the development of their book.

True to form, my first acknowledgment is to my wife, my best friend, and my partner in life, Sheila.

But I obviously owe so much of my success to the people who have partnered with me in business and in life. In fact, I see them as part of the Master Plan for me.

Deb Bricker has been my capable and devoted associate since "Day Two" in the life of El Dorado Holdings, Inc. She has been mentioned several times in this book, but she deserves one more mention here.

Roy McKay and Foster Friess have inspired me from the day I met them—Roy, because he never gives up, and Foster, because he gives and gives.

My amazing mentors have included Virgil Haley, John Tufts, Sr., Dr. Bill Burch, Dr. James Dobson, R. C. "Dick" Cline, Dr. Les Parrot, and Dr. David Le Shana, and, of course, Dr. Bill Bright.

All of my team members from my wholesale distribution days to my real estate ventures today have been important people in my life. I especially want to thank Betty Dalton, Sue Ann Dean,

David Elcyzyn, Ed Jessup, Sam Holman, James Walsh, Dal Ward, Nolan Chandler, Sue Buescher, and Denise Organ.

My partners, Monty Ortman, Dr. James Little, John Tufts, Sr., and all of those who have put their trust in me have earned my gratitude.

Several people have been involved in this book, including Stan Toler who has offered his invaluable insights for several years; Zig Ziglar, who kept telling me, "You have to write a book;" Sharon Lechter, who has brought her wisdom and guidance to the project from the perspective of an acclaimed bestselling author; and has supported me in updating and revising the original book into this edition. Steve Gottry, who has pushed me to focus on the purpose for this book as he crafted my ideas into carefully chosen words that express my heart. And to you, for taking the time to read them.

• • • • •

ABOUT THE AUTHOR AND THE HORATIO ALGER SOCIETY

In 1987, Mike co-founded El Dorado Holdings, Inc., a Phoenix-based land and development company with Monty Ortman and a total staff of one, Deb Bricker.

Over the years, Mike and El Dorado have faced numerous challenges and economic downturns, but the company has weathered each and every storm and is one of the area's largest private landholding companies, with assets exceeding one billion dollars. Mike attributes his success to his faith in God, his ability to surround himself with people smarter than himself, his strong relationships (both business and personal), and his solid belief in the words of his friend and mentor, Zig Ziglar: "You can get everything in life you want, if you help enough other people get what they want."

Mike Ingram

Mike is extremely passionate about giving back to his community and his country. He is committed to a number of business and civic organizations, including the Arizona Commerce Authority, Arizona-Mexico Commission, Barrow Neurological Foundation (Emeritus), Translational Genomics Research

Institute Foundation, C. M. Russell Museum, Shikar Safari Club International Foundation, and the National Cowboy and Western Heritage Museum. He is also actively involved with Pinnacle Forum.

    Today Mike is involved with the National Rifle Association, the Congressional Sportsman Foundation, a bi-partisan endeavor to promote conservation, Safari Club International, the World War II Museum, Gary Sinise Foundation, Shikar Safari Foundation. He also serves at the pleasure of the Secretary of Interior on the International Wildlife Conservation Council.

    Yes, Mike is an avid sportsman including hunting and fishing in the great outdoors while promoting the North American Game Conservation Model. A fact that few people are aware of is that funding for most, if not all, of the states' conservation programs are paid through excise tax on hunting and fishing licenses or associated equipment. The public reaps the benefit of being able to enjoy this country's bountiful wildlife through fees paid by hunters and fishermen. Mike believes today we enjoy more wildlife than ever before in North America due to the great conservation management programs carried out by the game and fish personnel in every state. He is quick to give thanks to those in the field who serve and protect.

Mike's passion for patriotism is embodied in several of his favorite quotes, including one from Ronald Reagan: "Freedom is never more than one generation away from extinction," and by John Quincy Adams: "Children should be educated and instructed in the principles of Freedom." And another by Winston Churchill who modified the original quote from George Santayana to state "Those who fail to learn from history are condemned to repeat it."

A framed quote by Dr. Robert Schuller hangs near the door of Mike's office. It's titled "The Laminated Principle," and it reads:

You Make a Promise – and Deliver.

You Accept an Assignment – and Fulfill It.

You Attempt Something "Impossible" —

and Pull it Off.

Finally, year after year, maybe decade after decade, you have applied one accomplishment on top of another, one achievement over another—promises kept and commitments fulfilled. Your reputation is like a laminated beam that has durability and power. People believe in you. They take you at your word. They'll sign a contract with you because they know you are going to deliver.

These words have guided Mike Ingram's life.

Mike and his wife, Sheila, reside in Phoenix, Arizona, and have six children, twenty-one grandchildren and eleven great grandchildren.

• • • • •

ABOUT THE HORATIO ALGER SOCIETY:

In recognition of his life's work and dedication to others, Mike Ingram was a 2019 recipient of the Horatio Alger Award. He was presented with the Horatio Alger Award and inducted as a lifetime Member of the Horatio Alger Association at a special induction ceremony at a three-day celebration held in Washington, D.C. on April 4 - 6, 2019.

As shared on its website, "The Horatio Alger Association of Distinguished Americans, Inc., a 501(c) (3) nonprofit educational organization, was established in 1947 to dispel the mounting belief among our nation's youth that the American Dream was no longer attainable.

The Association bears the name of the renowned author Horatio Alger, Jr., whose tales of overcoming adversity through unyielding perseverance and basic moral principles captivated the public in the late 19th century. The organization's founder, Dr. Kenneth Beebe, in close association with Dr. Norman Vincent Peale, hoped to inspire individual Americans to reach their highest potential, thereby strengthening American society as a whole. They created the Association to recognize men and women of outstanding achievement as a way to remind Americans of the limitless possibilities that exist through the free-enterprise system.

The Horatio Alger Association of Distinguished Americans is dedicated to the simple but powerful belief that hard work, honesty and determination can conquer all obstacles. The Association honors the achievements of outstanding leaders who have accomplished remarkable successes in spite of adversity by bestowing upon them the Horatio Alger Award and inducting them as lifetime Members. Since 1947, more than 700 distinguished individuals from all walks of life and diverse professional backgrounds have received the Horatio Alger Award and lifetime membership in the Association. There are currently more than 300 living Members, including ten Members from Canada.

Horatio Alger Members support promising young people with the resources and confidence needed to overcome adversity and pursue their dreams through higher education. Thanks to their generosity, in 2018 the Association awarded more than $16 million in undergraduate and graduate need-based scholarships across the United States and Canada and provides college support and mentoring services to its Scholars. Since 1984, the Association has awarded more than $175 million in college scholarships to more than 25,000 deserving young people."

For more Information about the Horatio Alger Society visit https://horatioalger.org/.

The Master Plan

Mike is honored and proud to join the distinguished recipients of the Horatio Alger Award, including many of his friends such as:

Foster Friess
Glenn Stearns
John Elway
Reba McEntire
Dennis Washington
Mark Victor Hansen
Michael Shannon
Harvey Mackay
John Grundhofer
Larry Ruvo
Tom Brokaw
Harold Hamm
T. Denny Sanford
R.C. Slocum
Matthew Rose
T. Boone Pickens
John Maxwell
Marcia Taylor
Justice Clarence Thomas
Roger Staubach
And many more!"